Scribbles from the Edge

Liz Hurley

Mudlark's Press

Cover artwork "Hilda" by Duane Bryers. Copyright
Brown & Bigelow.

Publisher: Mudlark's Press

ISBN-13: 9780993218002

"Those who find themselves ridiculous, sit down next to me"

James

Contents Page

Contents Page 7

Introduction 11

Wallpaper paste and black tie and so   another year begins 13

The surprising   beauties of Par Beach 17

Logistics is a doddle for mothers 21

Valentine's Day 25

Pomp, circumstance and sneaky shopping sprees 27

Am I a believer? 31

Bibliotherapy or the power of a good book 35

Senile old duffers? 39

Driving to Norfolk 43

Dog poo 47

Which is better,   rugby or football? 51

Time for me to grow a backbone 55

Harry the rubbish gun dog and his rubbisher handler! 59

I am now the proud owner of a new coat 63

Another rugby season comes to an end 67

Filthy, rotten,   cowardly thieves 69

A Year of Celebrations begins 71

Never ever make reading a chore for   children .. 73

The fun you can have when you say yes! 77

St Austell needs   another supermarket but where shall we put it? 81

My Olympic   highlights 85

How to improve   British sports 89

Riptides and weaver fish – a memorable day at the seaside 93

Walking the Saints Way with dogs,   dragons and monsters 97

Saying yes lands me in deep water 101
Helping those who help themselves and helping those
that can't..105
Take it on the chin and fail 109
Fudge failures and the Royal Cornwall Show 113
I don't like "emmets"...117
Saying one thing, meaning another...........................121
A rant on rude visitors...125
Farewell little school...129
This time saying yes lands me in shallow water......133
When it comes to childcare we are all in it together 137
The Glories of October 141
The Joy of Science...145
Walks with Harry..149
What Scottish 16 year olds can teach us.................151
Game pie and free food..155
What did I want to be when I grew up.....................159
Words fail me..163
Happy birthday to Us!..167
One for the birds 171
A sports stadium for Cornwall.................................175
Every wants a piece of me 179
We're just a little bookshop 183
Let's meet those low expectations 185
Is a kindle the end of the world?..............................189
Ode to Joy 191
The new online world 195
Exploding stupid cars..199
What makes a perfect school?..................................203
Looking pretty not stupid...207
Rubbish!...211
A Cornish Brigadoon 215
Writing and reading for The Cornish Guardian.......217
It's beginning to look a lot like Christmas...............221
Merry Christmas 225

Introduction

This book is a collection of columns that I have been writing for The Cornish Guardian. They roughly run in a seasonal order but they are selected from various years, so you might spot events next to each other that occurred years apart. They may include the odd rant and hopefully a few more laughs but I hope that you enjoy them and get a sense of what living in Cornwall is like when you are trying to run your own business and bring up children. You may learn something useful although I doubt it

Hilda

The lovely lady on the front cover is a character called Hilda. Isn't she a card! She was painted back in the 50s by Duane Bryers for the Calendar Company, Brown and Bigelow. When I first saw her I fell in love, she epitomizes what I strive for.

Have fun. Seize the Day. Say Yes. Who cares what you look like or what people will say?

Wallpaper paste and black tie and so another year begins

Oh dear God. So there I was, it was 5pm and I had almost finished a very challenging day of wallpapering when my phone rang. "Hi, tonight's do? Turns out it's going to be black tie and it's kicking off earlier than we realised so we're picking you up at 6.30. Sorry. See you in a bit." So now I had 90 minutes to finish the walls, wash and find a suitable outfit. Right now I know what you're thinking, if you're a lady you're wondering if I had my party frocks back from the drycleaners, how was I going to style my hair with wallpaper paste in it and that 90 minutes was going to be cutting it fine. If you're a gentleman you're wondering if I hung the paper with a plumb line. Gentlemen, I will address your concerns in a minute but more important things were afoot. Even if my frocks were back from the imaginary cleaners (oh how I would love to have that many dresses) they still wouldn't fit after a wonderfully indulgent Christmas.

Panicking, I finished the walls (a wee bit slap dash) ran for the bathroom and then attacked my wardrobe. The joy of having no clothes is that it doesn't take you long to realise that you truly have nothing to wear. Finally, I went for a full length skirt in brown silk and a matching top. Top was a wraparound and skirt had a drawstring waist; gentleman you may be all at sea with these descriptions but the ladies will appreciate the expandable natures of these garment. I wasn't hugely confident of the outfit though because the last time I wore it Steve said I looked like a Tudor milkmaid. And not the Benny Hill sort but the pestilence and poverty sort. Hey ho. I had just enough time to get a face on, look at the wallpaper, wince a bit at some of the edgings, kiss Steve and children goodnight before my ride whisked me away to a Burns Night party held at Pentewan Sands.

I relaxed back into the car thinking all my problems were over when one of the girls in the car asked "Do you reel?" Seemed a bit of a personal question and quite frankly I only start reeling after the third bottle's been opened and I wasn't going to tell her that, but then the horror dawned on me, she meant highland dancing, that sort of reel. Maybe my choice of three inch heels was not such a good wardrobe call after all.

I've got to say though that I had a fabulous time, my friend's husband hates dancing whilst she is fabulous at it, so we spent lot of time dashing off to the bar at the start of each dance. He was clearly more practiced at avoidance than I am as I kept being encouraged to join in. For a change the men on our table were exceptional dancers and I have never spent an evening apologising so much. I can dance, but I don't quite get left, right

14

and clockwise so once I've learnt a thing I'm fine but for the first few movements of every piece I was joining wrong sets, going backwards when I should have gone forward and stripping the willow with the wrong partner, and it was a far more sedate Strip the Willow than I remember. At school it seemed to be a contest to see who could swing the girls the furthest or make them fall over or show their knickers. And on the subject of knickers showing, some of the gentlemen last night needed to wear their sporrans a bit lower. We didn't know where to look when those kilts started flying!

All in all I met a lovely group of people, made a fool of myself in public, ate great food, yummy haggis and raised many a happy dram to the man himself. As for the wallpaper, well I'm tidying that up today.

The surprising beauties of Par Beach

It's easy to overlook what we have on our doorstep but I've recently learnt to love Par Beach. Until last year, the only time I went there was to litter pick with the school, it was always cold and drizzly, the work was dirty and boring and I would trudge away aching and wet. Then we got Harry, an exuberant Springer (is there any other type?) and we started to look around for walks; our warehouse is in Par, so the beach was an obvious choice. It's never going to be a beach I use to sunbathe on or swim in but there's so much else to do.

Throughout the day, the life of the beach ebbs and flows. The sun rises on fishermen digging for lugworms and riders stretching their horses as they plunge through the waves; dog walkers give way to sun worshipers as the day progresses, children spill onto the beach after school and then kite surfers tear along the surf, blowing a day's work out of their hair. The sun sets and barbeques are lit and eventually the beach returns to the wildlife. At low tide in winter there are cockles and razor clams to be harvested. In summer the paths running through the sand dunes are drenched in the scent of dog roses and gorse.

For my part I just walk Harry and thought I'd seen all there was to see. In fact if you give me a grain of sand I can probably tell you which part of the beach it comes from. Of course there's not just the beach front. There's a great walk over the coast path to Polkerris and if the tide is low enough you can scramble back over the rocks going along Boolies beach. If you're lucky (and Harry is not nearby) you can spot all sorts of wildlife. I clocked 22 different birds once; I couldn't name them all mind you.

In fact it was my ignorance of what I was looking at that prompted me to go on a free bird spotters walk hosted by the Cornwall Wildlife Trust (CWT). I turned up with binoculars and without Harry and discovered so much more about Par Beach. Did you know that there are otters there! We walked around the pond and cut through the holiday park through the wood (there's a wood!) and came out by the river where kingfishers have been spotted. There was so much that I had never seen before (I tend to avoid the pond as Harry and geese would be a lethal and noisy combination.) We also saw some of the work carried out by the Friends of Par Beach, a group of volunteers, who, like volunteers the world over, work hard but keep quiet.

I discovered this walk in a small square book published by the council of all countryside events occurring in

18

Cornwall both free and paid. So, many thanks, to the Friends of Par Beach, to the CWT for providing the fascinating walk and the council for putting together the free guide (try your local library or TIC for a copy). Harry and I will now explore new pastures with greater knowledge.

Logistics is a doddle for mothers

A parcel delivered by City Link couldn't be delivered through my letterbox so I was left a handy ransom note instead. There was a telephone number to dial that would rarely be answered and, when it was, I had the option to decipher the unique number scrawled across the card in order to re-book a delivery. It would generally take a few attempts, "I don't know, try S, No? Try 5 then" and so on until my parcel details would pop up. I really don't know why my house number and postcode isn't enough. With DHL they use barcodes which I thought were easy to read until someone in the Truro depot told me that when they get into the depot they are reassigned new barcodes and sometimes the two barcodes don't get paired together properly. Anyway, an agreed date to re-deliver would be then duly ignored and another "failed to deliver" would drop through the letterbox with the message that the parcel had been returned to sender and to please contact sender. Details about who the sender may have been remain unknown. A slightly metaphysical quandary.

Lost parcels are just as much fun as undelivered ones. The depot can't locate the parcel so do you want to make a claim? Please specify what you have lost. Tricky as you don't know what it is, so conveniently you can't make a claim. I was once asked if I knew what it was? It was Christmas, was I expected to phone up everyone I knew and ask if they had sent a present to my son? Can you imagine how awkward that conversation would be?

"Hi, did you send us a present?"
"No."
"OK"
"Should I have sent you a present?"

But I have the solution. If a parcel company is having a logistics issue they should ask a mother to come in and sort it out.

Last week after rugby skills session in Truro I collected my eldest and his mate, and headed to Lanivet roundabout to rendezvous with his mate's mother whereby she handed over my second son who had been staying with friends near her, as well as eldest son's bags left behind from a sleepover and I handed over her son. At these moments we tend to grin at each other, just check that we have the right amount of bags and the correct children in the car and drive off. No journey is wasted as we pick up from others and drop off along the way. This swapping of children also means that parents can go to work whilst other parents look after a whole brood. Being self-employed may mean that you work very odd hours but it also means you can be pretty flexible.

So far none of us have been forced to phone up a faceless depot and try to describe what our son looks like and could they please try to redeliver him, along with his bags and do that before 10.00 so that we can go to the beach.

Towards the end of summer there is the general "Whose shoes are these?" and the round of e-mails asking if anyone has seen a raincoat and gradually, by the first week of September, all is back in place and we can all collapse. So DHL next time you can't find my parcel give your Mother a call and ask her if she knows where it is!

Valentine's Day

As you are reading this I should like you to picture me under mounds of flowers, surrounded by boxes of chocolates and lots of little treats. I am also imaging myself like this but I'm not sure what that would look like as once again it hasn't happened. Valentine's Day is an annual disappointment for many I'm sure but I always feel aggrieved when I do have a chap but that his attitude is that Valentine's Day is nothing more than a cynical, commercial enterprise to make us spend more money on one particular day of the year. That argument would hold more water if he did lots of romantic things throughout the rest of the year, or picked a little posy from the garden for me. Curiously though none of these things happen either.

Despite my customary disappointment in the middle of February, the year has started pretty well. The resolutions that Steve and I made have, remarkably, been kept to. I went for a scattergun approach in the hope that I would be able to stick to at least one resolution and this appears to be the trick. The resolution I'm having the most success with was "have more fun." It seems a daft thing to resolve to do but sometimes I just get bogged down by the laundry, vat returns, customer queries, the school run and so on that I forget to just enjoy myself. So anyway, I've been to a Burn's Night, caught up with my family, watched the Chinese State Circus, been out for lunch with friends, a huge walk with great company, cheered on rugby, football and cross country teams. I've gone foraging for mussels and had a lovely cheap supper, I've redecorated my front room with help from my neighbour and I've gradually started to remodel the house into something that works for a growing family. I've even managed to lose weight, drink less and do more exercise!

To be honest this is a thing unheard of but I'm thoroughly enjoying myself. So how are you doing? If you are trying to give up smoking then I have so much respect for you, addictions are awful things to get over and I imagine the trick is, if you have a smoke not to think you've failed and give up but to just keep trying. But then what do I know, one of my resolutions was to give up sweets altogether which I should have known was a non-starter.

It's going to be even harder this week as the shop re-opens for the season and I'll have a glorious   sweet shop on hand just across the way from me. Oh get behind me Satan and take your Jellied Fruits with you! It doesn't help that "eat less sweets" is in direct conflict with "have more fun." Oh well, got to crack on, that laundry doesn't wash itself and neither does the dog. And if I do get flowers for Valentine's I'll owe my darling husband an enormous apology.

Pomp, circumstance and sneaky shopping sprees

It's my fault. I'm sorry. I won't do it again I promise. The boys were lined up for their last rugby match, a cold wind was blowing and I did it, I went and said "at least it's not raining!" 'twasn't five minutes before the heavens opened and we ran for our cars. Well we did, the boys had to play on slippy grass and rock hard ground. Bad mother.

It's been a lovely run of weather; in fact it's been the hottest April on record which makes me wonder what July and August might be like. A friend came back from Portugal where they had had seven days of rain to find everyone in the UK browner than she was. That's not right. Well, it's not right but it is nice. It was great to have a good sunny Easter and I'm so glad that it lasted long enough for everyone to enjoy their street parties and for all of those mad fools that flocked to London to stand in massive crowds I'm glad that it was dry for them too.

I really enjoyed the wedding, I'll be honest and confess that I didn't watch it live, I needed to get new wetsuits for the boys and I figured the roads would be empty during the actually ceremony. I can smugly announce that I was right and I nipped over to Newquay in record time and then came back and watched the recording. It was fabulous, I love all the pomp and circumstance, I'm not one for doffing my cap or thinking anyone is "better" than me but I do love to see celebrations and to see our nation at its most majestic best. I belted out Bread of Heaven along with the congregation, wondered aloud why Sarah's daughters couldn't afford mirrors and loved the inspirational trees in the cathedral. How beautiful were they!? Their tall towering columns were radiant against the marble columns of the cathedral, I thought it was inspired. I don't think some potted plants in Hurley Books would have the same affect but it did make me want to transform the shop into an arboretum. From trees to books – a perfect match.

I didn't expect the boys to like it but they were equally taken with the whole affair, they were most impressed with the regimented marching and had lots of questions "Did the Queen have a gun in her bag?" What if Katherine said no?" "If Harry shot William would the police shoot Harry?" "Were the Royal Lifeguards from Newquay?" "Can we have an Aston Martin" and so on.

It just made me realise how great the Olympics are going to be. Now they ARE people who are "better" than me and I'll really be pleased and proud to cheer them on. I tried to buy tickets but found the whole procedure so hit and miss and rather expensive that I'll wait until the autumn when they offer up the spares. I'd love to take the boys to the opening or closing ceremonies and a medals day, I'm not sure about sailing because as much as they love it, it is a rather difficult spectator sport. Steve's concerned that numbers for beach volleyball may be low so feels that we should go and support that event. Steve also thinks that I was born yesterday.

Even if we don't get to see anything live we can still watch on television and enjoy all that will be going on. I can't wait and I just know what a success it will be, because my god the wedding was perfect so we know we can pull off huge events and have the entire world look at us and cheer.

Am I a believer?

Am I a believer? Probably, I think we all are a bit but what we believe in differs wildly. A few years back I was at a children's carol concert when a guest preacher told a joke that pretty much let the Father Christmas identity out of the bag. Little children looked confused, older children looked on in amazement and parents were livid. My main annoyance was who was this man to say that his belief system was any more valid than my sons'?

There seem to be those that believe and won't listen to alternatives as they "know" that they are right. Then there are those that believe that their belief system is no such thing but a rigorously proven scientific system and won't listen to alternatives and in fact will dismiss out of hand beliefs that just seem too hard to swallow. Then there are the "sit on the fence types" that seem to believe nothing and know nothing preferring not to make their mind up. I probably belong to the sceptics and fence sitters more than the believers. But until last week I was quite happy knowing that the fastest thing in the universe was light because Einstein had proved it. Now it looks like that might be under question and I love it. I love it when rock solid absolutes are shaken. Of course at these moments, scientists quite happily declare that nothing is certain and in fact true scientists regularly say the world is less known than we think, but those that believe in science find that their belief system can also be shaken. It seems that scientists are only right until they are proved wrong, alternative thinkers are considered wrong until scientists can prove them right.

Now, if we are going to put gravity and *feng shui* in a boxing ring I know which one I am going to back and not just because gravity has its feet on the ground and *feng shui* doesn't like the alignment of the corner it's sitting in. I'm backing gravity because there has been a whole heap of proven research into it for centuries and my front door faces south and is painted red and I still haven't made a fortune.

It's easy to mock alternative ways at looking at the world but often we rush to advance our knowledge and leave perfectly good discoveries behind. The best way to get rid of ulcerating sores? Bind them up with maggots. Totally mediaeval but it works, however, by the same token those in the know back then thought that bleeding was also a great cure for all ills.

So what don't I believe in? Well *feng shui* for a start and being able to talk to the dead. I don't believe that aliens built the pyramids, I don't disbelieve in aliens, they just don't strike me as the jobbing mason sort. I don't believe in astrology and I don't believe in fortune telling. I don't believe in fairies but sea monsters are fair game. I think people are just bags of water, chemicals and electrical impulses so I'll remain open minded on dowsing, acupuncture, homeopathy and chakras.

I do believe that there are more thing in heaven and hell than are dreamt of in our philosophy so I'm going to remain open minded and just because I believe doesn't mean I'm right and just because someone can't prove a thing doesn't mean that they are wrong. And as for Father Christmas – well his existence is without doubt.

Bibliotherapy or the power of a good book

Reading back on last week's column I've noticed that I might have come across as a bit odd doing my homework in graveyards and reading in cathedrals. The thing is I love those big quiet spaces. Maybe it shouldn't have been such a shock to my friends and family that I became a Librarian because whilst I might be a noisy thing most of the time, once I have a book in my hands I want to get lost in that book. In the past when I had the luxury of reading for days I could get well and truly into a book and would often end up talking like the characters. That would be acceptable when it was Austen although one might opine that it was a trifle formal, but daft when reading Arthurian fiction verily forsooth! Some days I would emerge from a book bleary eyed and at odds with the reality around me, other times I would dream about the characters, drive along thinking of solutions or catch myself crying over something that wasn't real.

The power of a story is nothing new, in fact it's as old as it gets but now that power has been given a name – bibliotherapy. Coined in the States by our cousins who do love their therapies, bibliotherapy is based on the curative powers of the right book. I'm a bit of a stiff upper lip sort of girl (when I'm not blubbing over soppy bits in books) but even I can see that this new therapy has a point. Well as I said it's not new is it? Just that it's been formally acknowledged and given a name.

The idea is that the right book can help unlock all sorts of internal problems. Sometimes it can help get your own situation in perspective; reading about the atrocities in Rwanda makes your concerns about credit card debts more manageable. That's not to say that your concerns are not relevant, it simply helps you see them in a different light and once you can do that you can start to deal with them. It's very easy when you hit a huge problem to believe that it's an insurmountable wall, even worse when it seems like that wall is falling down on top of you. Other areas in which books can help are where they share a similar theme to the one you are dealing with; if you are supporting someone who is dying then it's easy again to feel isolated, reading about someone who has gone through the same process can help people especially with what's to come. The unknown is pretty terrifying for all of us and it's nice to have someone hold your hand in the privacy of your own mind.

My favourite kind of therapy is the one of escapism. When the children were babies and I seemed to have become stuck in some sort of biological nightmare and daytime TV, the stories that took me away from it all were the best. Who cared what Tinky Winky was doing when my spaceship was about to crash into an alien colony? Rather than watch some ninny tell me that a pile of old tat might make £80 at auction I could ponder the wonders of the Fibonacci sequence and when it seemed like Cornwall may never have sunshine again I was sunning myself on the Argentine Plains watching Polo ponies race up and down. I'd always find that when I put the book down the world seemed a calmer place. True, the mess, the chaos, the worries were all exactly where I had left them but suddenly they weren't the wall they had seemed and I was able to hop over them.

If you've ever read a book that has really helped you out of a jam or have a book that you always turn to when things get hairy I'd love to hear about it. enquiries@hurleybooks.co.uk or Hurley Books or Facebook. By the same token if you want some advice as to what book to read, get in touch.

Senile old duffers?

I've been thinking about people who are a generation or two older than me. I can't call them the elderly because I may get a clip around the ear and also because, as time is a one way conveyor belt, I too, will one day become old and I don't wish to be described as elderly either. Age of course is all relative, my sons already think I'm ancient and see little distinction between someone in their 40s and someone in their 70s, even 30 year olds are looking a bit over the hill but from my point of view I view old as being retired, to keep this clear I also view middle aged as retired.

The reason for my ponderings is because I've been watching how older people get spoken to. I know dementia is an issue for some but it's not something that gets handed out with the bus pass, so why do I keep hearing younger people speaking to older people as though they are dim, foreigners. Slowly, loudly and in words of few syllables. People in their seventies grew up with rationing still being in place, they saw society structures fall apart and reshape itself through the 50s. In the 60s they exploded. They decided that liberation was something that everyone should benefit from. They do owe us an apology for the awful fashions of the seventies. They have lived through lots of wars, strikes and recessions, massive technological breakthroughs, they witnessed man first leaving the planet, so if they don't know who Cheryl Cole is and don't consider Robbie Williams a tortured individual let's not assume that they are senile old duffers eh?

On one occasion I accompanied my mother whilst she was house hunting, the agent kept talking to me, saying "your mother will find it's nice and close to the shops." In front of her! When we left I asked mum if that was normal. Apparently it's completely run of the mill. Now what I don't get is that as you retire and become "invisible", it must really hack a person off. So why don't they do something about it? They are the baby boomers after all and we know there's a lot of them about and they were pretty militant in their time. As they look forward to tiny pensions, and extortionate fuel bills why don't they get together and rise up? Imagine if a political party was formed solely to address the needs of the retiring population, I bet they'd do well in the elections. Even the concept of retiring is undergoing a massive shift. It used to mean stop working and live for another 10 or 20 years. Now we seem to go on for another 40. Forty years of retirement? That's bonkers. We have a burgeoning post 60 population who really need to be addressed head on. As a society we just can't afford it but we're going to have to do something. My bet is that if politicians stopped ignoring them and starting talking to them we might be able to shake things up a bit.

In this culture we seem to venerate the young and the money-makers. I see nothing wrong with that in moderation but it seems daft to ignore the experience gained from knocking about over the decades. It also seems massively disrespectful to assume that because someone can't open their e-mail that they must have lost their IQ along with their last haircut. But what do I know I'm just a whipper snapper. Honest.

Driving to Norfolk

Well this week I faced the joys of a long distance car trip. Is there any other sort when you're leaving Cornwall but as I was headed for Norfolk it was quite a stretch, 400 miles in fact. Like all journeys it started with lots of familiar landscape that seemed to make it feel as though you weren't actually getting anywhere, until we get to Exeter the route is identical for any journey that involves leaving Cornwall and familiarity breeds boredom. I know some people bemoan the advent of electronic gizmos and hanker for the days of eye spy but eye spy can only last for about 30 minutes by the most Enid Blyton of families. For the more Simpsons type of family, eye spy usually degenerates into accusations of cheating and tortuous rules after 10 minutes. I'm sure I'm not the only person to be amazed by the convoluted rules that siblings will suddenly invent to ensure that their brother fails to win his round. So it is with great joy that I load up their devices with story books, films, music and games and then listen to Radio 4 in peace and quiet as the car steadily chews up the miles.

We did of course play the odd game of yellow car, fives, car cricket and eye spy. The occasional diversions were supplied by other road users and oddities in the country-side. For a while we were entertained by a stunt plane that was practising loop the loops, dives and backwards flips, he was so impressive that I'm amazed that the M4 wasn't littered with cars that had all run into each other as the drivers gazed at the skies rather than the tarmac ahead. As we moved onto the M25 we kept an eye out for Windsor Castle, as soon as we spot it we know that we are on the last leg of the journey so it's always a great moment. The M11 provides two tunnels with which to hold our breath and then we are onto the A11.

Travelling to Norfolk is like Cornwall in many ways. The motorway peters out and suddenly you are welcomed by empty duel carriage ways (I'm not including Saturdays) and the world seems to drop away from you. You pass through Suffolk or Devon and suddenly hit a single lane carriage way, invariably this is crowded and you wonder where all the traffic has come from. The stretch in Norfolk goes on for many, many miles and is long and straight; invariably people crash their cars, tempted by high speed overtaking and so the road network grinds to a halt as it cuts through MOD land and there's no left or right turn. Thankfully we pass along the stretch unhindered by delays and reach Norfolk with ease. Like Cornwall, Norfolk is not on the way to anywhere, no one passes through Norfolk on their journey to somewhere else and so it has that sleepy not bothered air that Cornwall has. Unlike Cornwall you can actually see Norfolk. Gone are the steep banks on either side of the road, the tree lined tunnels the reinforced hedges, instead the road drifts over to sandy curbs sown with wild poppies that spill onto the huge flat fields that stretch away to the ever present sky laid out in all its glory. I know I'm waxing lyrical but I do miss the sky here in Cornwall.

The return journey had everything that we had missed on the trip up, the fights, the hot weather, the many traffic jams but it also had the sense of excitement as we ticked off the Tavistock turning, Gilbert the Goblin's house, the hedgehog bridge and finally our own road and Steve and Harry waiting with huge grins. Journeys are about the travelling; to the destination but most importantly about coming home at the end.

Dog poo

Did you ever see the Billy Connolly sketch where he was talking about his trip to Australia? He was talking about all the vicious things that could kill you and was particularly taken with marine life and in particular the Box Jellyfish, a creature that could kill a man a hundred times over. His main concern was the naming of this savage beast, box jellyfish "They gift wrap the feckers!" I have to point out that he didn't say feckers, he was a wee bit more Anglo Saxon. Anyway, it was the whole concept of gift wrapping a lethal weapon that made me wonder about other inappropriate gift wrap items. Dog poo for example, why do people feel the need to gift wrap it? I despair of the amount of times I see neat little bags littered all around the countryside.

This really got my goat the other day when I got out of the car and within ten metres of the car park sitting on top of a large granite boulder was a little blue poo bag neatly tied up and sitting in pride of place. Who does this? What is the thinking behind it? Did they think the boulder needed highlighting? They hadn't left it to collect later as there was no car present and was still there an hour later. If they considered poo to be so completely offensive that it needs wrapping up why the hell don't they take it home with them? Was it a protest because there was no bin provided? What's to protest about? It's your dog and his poo. Clear it up yourself and take it away, don't expect someone else to do it for you! It's great when bins are provided and I do like not having to drive home with little piles of gift wrapped poo but I don't leave them in pride of place to register my annoyance.

I can't make up my mind if this person's actions were better or worse than the idiot that gift wraps the poo and then hurls it into the hedgerow to hang forlornly from the branches like a toxic tree decoration. Actually, I can make my mind up, this is worse; it offends the eye but can't be reached and removed. It adds nothing but plastic to the ecosystem and shows such lack of concern for the landscape and environment that I wonder why these people even have a dog.

So is a plastic bag parked on a stone or hanging from a tree better or worse that a pile of mess that hasn't been gift wrapped? Hard to say really, at least un-wrapped it can decompose but if you stand in it or the children fall in it it's an entirely different matter. I walk a lot around here and I can safely say that I always know when I am approaching a car park because the incidence of uncollected poo goes through the roof, or all over the path, pick your own analogy. I have seen owners so lazy that they open their car doors let the dog jump out run around, do his bit and then they call them back to the car. These people should have their dogs removed immediately. How dare they! These public spaces are for everyone to enjoy and it's hard to enjoy a place covered in poo. No one who is able to drive a car is unable to get out of it and remove the poo from the main path.

So what to do? If you're going to gift wrap it then take it home or carry it until you find a bin. If you're not going to pick it up then flick it into the undergrowth as advised by the Forestry Commission, it will rot down, out of sight and not underfoot. Can I just say though, that if you walk your dog on a beach then always, bag it and remove it? Nowhere is out of bounds to children's bare feet in summer.

Which is better, rugby or football?

Right I am about to stick my neck out and get shot down in a hail of bullets. I will be publicly pilloried, I will shop with a bag over my head but here goes.   Football is a more skilful game than rugby. There I've said it! Even typing it has made me look over my   shoulder to see if anyone saw what I wrote. Clearly this is not the best county in which to make such a statement but I'm afraid that's how I see it. Now as you know both my sons play and love rugby and if I had to choose to watch a rugby or football match I would always choose the rugby match. I prefer Rugby but if I had to say which is the most skilful then of course it's football.

Those guys are incredibly fit, the spend the whole 90 minutes running after the ball, there's no stopping for rucks, mauls, scrums and line outs – it is constant chasing across the field and the whole time you are trying to control a ball with just your feet. Those feet that you are also trying to run with. Just watching the players on TV and their amazing ball control skills is outstanding. Of course Rugby is a skilful game and yes rugby players are stronger, as to who is fitter I'm not sure but as to which requires the greater skill, then it's football.

Recently I heard a daft argument about how a football player wouldn't last three minutes on a rugby pitch but then neither would a cricketer, a sprinter or a swimmer. Rugby is a hard, tough game and very exciting to watch but it's not for everyone.

This past week I've been watching a lot of football, not my choice but everyone else is watching it and as I've always said any sport is great to watch when it is being played by the very best (except golf – how can you watch golf? Playing it is fun, watching it is an exercise in tedium.) That said, football players are the biggest bunch of babies I have ever seen. I swear these guys will fall over a blade of grass if they think they can get the ref to award a penalty! They are not an impressive bunch and hardly act as role models for future sportsmen. Certainly they are very valuable assets to their club and if they are tackled it makes sense to stay on the ground and check if the bang has caused any serious damage but the tears and histrionics are pathetic.

One of the things that always amaze me about football fans though is the split in the types that attend. When you look into the crowd you see the laughter, the tears, the hope and pride all the very best in a nation supporting their country and then there are the idiots. The people that throw rubbish on the pitch, last night someone threw a smoke bomb onto the pitch! They had to stop the game as it got so bad that the goalie couldn't see the play of the ball. Why would anyone do that? They no doubt paid good money to get a seat and then they think it's fun to disrupt the game. For those players nothing is more important than the game they are playing and yet some wally comes along and halts play.

Beyond the pitch, football seems to bring out the worst in people, the violence, the racism, the sheer minded hooliganism. What is it about this game that attracts this behaviour when it doesn't happen in cricket or rugby? Anyway England play tonight and by the time you read this we are hopefully on our way to the next rounds. With or without the tears.

Time for me to grow a backbone

I was walking out of Tesco today when the newspaper front covers caught my eye. They were the ones that are face on at pram height and they were showing the mutilated face and body of Gaddafi from various angles with headlines such as "Don't Shoot" and "That's For Lockerbie." To be frank I was shocked and got as far as the car before I thought no that's really wrong and went back into the shop to see if I had really seen those images at the eye level of small children. Obviously Tesco has no power over what the papers print no matter how sensationalist and brutal, but they do have a say over how they are displayed. So I went over to customer services and pointed out that I thought those low level face on papers should be removed. The lady at customer services seemed unimpressed pointing out that children see far worse on their X Box.

Now I hate to come over all righteous and whatever but I was appalled. This was a real image of a man beaten and shot to death, with words pleading for his life right at the eye level of two to seven year olds. I was not concerned with the rights and wrongs of the disposal of a brutal dictator but with the sensibilities of children. I thought the X-Box argument was a red herring because very young children don't play the bloodier games and even if they do see them is that right? The customer advisor said she could raise it with a manager if I wanted?

I felt quite defeated and said yes if she could pass my complaint along that I would be grateful and I left the shop. I felt really bad, I didn't have the courage of my convictions to stand and wait for the manager but left feeling wholly out of step with the world. I got home and threw out a whinge on Facebook and was surprised with the number and speed of replies agreeing that it was out of order. Now these are my friends replying so you might expect them to agree with me – but then you wouldn't know my friends very well, they'd either politely ignored my compliant or point out why I was wrong.

Feeling encouraged by the mob rule I rang up Tesco to ask if there had been any follow up. Blow me down, Tesco had removed all those low level covers. What a result! But what lessons I learnt. First, have the courage of your convictions. Don't think you are out of step with the world. Maybe the rest of the world thinks that they are also out of step? What if we all turned round and said I don't like this. Maybe we could really improve things. The next thing I learnt was it was worth complaining because maybe Tesco had already received a complaint from someone else and were just waiting to see if anyone else complained. Or maybe one complaint was enough. And that's the next thing that I learnt. Great big companies will listen to individual issues and respond immediately so it's always worth airing your concerns rather than walking away thinking no one will listen. The old adage is true, the person that sees the problem is the person that should deal with the problem.

I'm not suggesting that I'm about to become some sort of campaigning zealot but if I see something I'm not impressed with I'm going to develop my backbone and go and have a word and if the first person I complain to seems unimpressed I'm going to stand by my feelings and go up a level.

Harry the rubbish gun dog and his rubbisher handler!

As some of you may know we have a springer spaniel going by the name of Harry. He's three years old now and I have always meant to get him trained properly, it is after all what he is bred to do, and after my column on prevarication the other week I finally picked up the phone and spoke to a trainer. On the phone Mel seemed very nice and we agreed to meet up and see if Harry was up to the grade. We met up at Minions and in reality she seemed every bit as nice as she had on the phone but it soon became apparent that it would be a question of whether I was up to the grade just as much as Harry!

So Harry and I got out of the car and instantly my heart sank. All around us were wild ponies and sheep, I'm afraid Harry is pretty good but not perfect and I was concerned that things might career down the pan before we got started. However, Mel agreed that they would be too distracting for him and we moved them on so that we could begin our work. At first Mel wanted to know what I'd taught Harry, we'd obviously already failed the ignoring sheep test. I explained that we'd only really done the basics but that Harry was pretty good at those. It turned out that he wasn't. I demonstrated how well Harry walked to heel, Mel pointed out that Harry was walking to heel when he felt like it because he liked my company not because he had been told to. The minute something more interesting came up, say a gorse bush or a butterfly, he was off. His recall was equally suspect. Yes, he did come back to me but not always, once again that passing gorse bush could be an attractive thing to a dog with clouds in his head. The stay command worked well although I had been doing it wrong. Apparently when you tell a dog to "stay" you must always return to him, you shouldn't call him to you because stay means just that. If I want him to sit in one spot and then come to me it's "Sit" and then "Come here". Or rather three blows on the whistle. Which I didn't have.

We then began to walk in circles and squares and figures of eight which I kept getting wrong, memories of my terrible attempts at dancing at Burn's Night earlier in the year came flooding back and Mel seemed quite bemused by someone that couldn't complete a figure of eight without getting lost. After that humiliation we progressed onto retrieval work, which Harry thought was great fun and acquitted himself fairly well. At the end of the session Mel thought that Harry had promise and I needed to do some homework so we went away happy with our progress. So far, he's walking to heel on the lead perfectly and off the lead he's pretty good except for the odd gorse bush. Sit and Stay are also working well but he seems to have nosed dived when it comes to retrieving. One thing at a time is going to have to be our motto. I'll let you know how we get on.

I am now the proud owner of a new coat

I am now the proud owner of a new coat. Much to the confusion of Steve, who thinks that I have more than enough coats already. But that's daft, I don't have a heavy weather coat and this is what I need. For the past few winters I have borrowed his, to his constant annoyance so I thought that this year I would finally get my own. As he pointed out I already have a rain mac but it's really just a light weight pretty shower coat. The sort for popping in and out of shops; not the sort for pushing through gorse bushes and withstanding sea spray, mud, gales and horizontal rain. I also have a lovely bright green wool coat but again, there's no way I'm taking that out on a dog walk and my jacket is not a coat no matter how much Steve tries to tell me it's the same thing.

It's like those men who say women have too many shoes. (I won't use Steve as an example again; poor thing will start to feel victimised, if his views coincide with these fictional male characters, well that's not my fault.) You know the type; he'll say why do you need more than one pair of shoes? Well really, what a thing to say? Who wears slippers on a dog walk, or wellies to work? Flip flops don't work in winter, walking boots are no good on the squash court, Stilettos are no good on the rugby pitch and rugby boots are rarely acceptable at the dinner table. So honestly, who only has one pair of shoes?

Anyway, my coat. It is not a thing of beauty but it is pretty practical. Imagine a waxed sheet of tarpaulin with a zip up the middle; now stop imagining because that's basically what it is. It is warm, wind proof and water proof, I wade through gorse bushes laughing and spit in the eye of the elements. It has all the functional attributes of a sheet of tarpaulin but it is also fair to say that it also has all the aesthetic appeal of a sheet of tarpaulin, albeit one with a zip up the middle, oh and lots of pockets. I bought it on eBay with a strict budget in mind, somewhere between stingy and parsimonious. As I was flicking through the pages my eyes kept resting upon beautiful ladies' Barbours lined with Liberty fabric and fitted belts. You can imagine that the minute Liberty and Barbour occur in the same description that the price tag will exceed parsimonious and as for the fur lined, down filled gilet that I fell in love with – oh dear! Instead I saw a long waxed men's jacket which looked just the ticket and also looked brand new. It was within my means and so I am now the proud owner of something that can withstand hurricanes. Of course as it is new it has the flexibility of a drainpipe but that will come. It took about a year to make my last wax comfortable but I didn't have a dog helping out last time.

Now I just need a new handbag. Oh dear, I've got to go, I can hear Steve choking in the background.

Another rugby season comes to an end

It seems hard to believe but another year has passed and the rugby season is finally over. It's been a rough year for the club having its club house vandalised and losing Paul but Lankelly Fowey aren't ones for giving up. My boys have turned out most weeks for training and matches, they have played in hail and driving rain, slid along mud slides, been gouged, thumped and tackled again and again and again but they loved every minute. I'm not sure how much fun it was for the coaches and parents who also turn out every week but for our sins we must enjoy watching our children try their hardest and sometimes succeeding.

So now that the rugby is over you'd think I'd get a rest but my youngest has decided that he wants to come running with me. The first time he came I tried to keep up with him which proved to be a massive mistake. Not only can I not run a mile yet, I'm also not Usain Bolt. Finn can not only run rings around me at speed he can do it for miles and miles. To make things more fun he has decided to lap me, to see how many miles he can run whilst I try to run just one. I'm not sure who is finding this fun. I know it's not me but I suspect by his grins and shouts of encouragement as he goes past that it might be him.

My eldest boy now having lost his weekly outlet for rage and violence has turned to his piano with gusto and no little amount of trepidation on behalf of his piano. His teacher was a bit concerned that he wasn't making much progress recently until we discovered that there was a language breakdown. Rachel was telling Thomas to look at a certain piece. Thomas did just that, he looked at it. For weeks he looked at it, and then went on to play his own pieces. Rachel has now stopped asking him to look but to actually play it and progress is being made.

Of course running and piano is not enough of an outlet for sporty kids so out come the surf boards and the sail boats and there goes the state of my car. I wish there wasn't this modern obsession with carpeted cars, the sand gets so wedged in and it never hoovers out – just more mess to learn to live with. I liked the old lino types where it all just sluiced out, dog hair, mud, sand, food, the whole lot swept out and then washed down.

So it's going to be a long sporty summer ahead of us, hopefully with lots of lovely sunshine and long sunny evenings. The children can go grab their bikes and ride their socks off and Steve and I will relax over a well-earned glass of something chilled. Cheers!

Filthy, rotten, cowardly thieves

I'm in a very bad mood. Some of you may know my brother John; he lived here in Cornwall for a few years and loved his time in Mevagissey. Eventually the siren calls of Norfolk pulled him home and he returned to Norwich with his sweetheart Katie and settled down and they now have a gorgeous little girl. I know, how amazing, John, a father! Anyway, he's a self-employed carpenter, a pretty good one even if I do say so myself, my hand built kitchen and panelled bathroom are just some testaments to this. It's hard work and despite his skill, like most manual jobs it's not always well paid, work can be on and off and financially, times can be tough. So imagine how awful it was for him to wake up one morning and discover that his van had been broken into and all his equipment had been cleared out.

The sheer front of these thieves is all the more shocking when you discover that he lives on a terrace without front gardens so the van was within feet of his front door and that of his neighbours. Even worse, because his little one was teething John was sleeping on the sofa right by the front door. The police called and explained that this appeared to be the work of a gang that had very smart methods at breaking in silently and removing gear quickly, poor John wasn't the only craftsman to wake up and discover their livelihood had been stolen.

The insults continued as he got in touch with his insurers, his car insurers said that they don't cover powered goods, his home contents insurers said they don't cover work equipment. So in the space of minutes John went from losing over a thousand pounds worth of tools to realising that they would not be replaced. He's worked years to build up his collection and as a self-employed workman he doesn't have access to a company pool of tools. His friends have rallied round and offered him their stuff but as he quietly puts it, his tools were for professional use not occasional DIY and he doesn't want to damage or wear out something offered in a generous spirit. And of course his mates that are also chippies need their own tools.

So now he has no work, no funds to replace his tools and he'll have to start from the bottom all over again. All this heartache and misery because some people out there are lazy, thieving, deeply, deeply unpleasant people. The police don't think they'll catch them and if they do John will never get his tools back or be properly recompensed and they will get minimal sentences.

There is something really wrong when it's the hardworking, honest types that lose out whilst the cheating, feckless sorts prosper. As I said I am in a bad mood.

A Year of Celebrations begins

It's been a pretty incredible week hasn't it? I think looking back this is going to be one of those summers that sticks out like 1976 or 1985. First we had the Olympic torch relay and then we had the Golden Jubilee and what struck me most on each occasion was how incredible it is when we all do something together with smiles on our faces. I don't think the torch procession really had much to do with our love of the Olympics and in the same way that I don't think our Jubilee celebrations were solely motivated from a love for the Queen. In fact, what I think both of them demonstrated was how proud we are of our country and our neighbourhoods.

How could you fail to be moved by watching all the pomp and ceremony process down the Mall or the grins from children as neighbours piled out onto the streets in the drizzle to have a party with each other? I have no problem with the monarchy so this may colour how I viewed the weekend but I thought it was marvellous, how often do we get to have a full on splurge where we just revel in how good we are. Too often we apologise for things or we look to blame others or we shrug our shoulders and say the country is rubbish but what can be done? But wow – just look at what we can achieve when we want to.

The celebrations were twofold in Mevagissey as it launched its first SeaFest (everything has to be Fest at the moment, have you noticed?) The RNLI and Coastguard were out in force, there was live music all day long and stalls and other events. Spread over two days the weather was kind on both and from all that I've heard the event was a huge success. The funds raised are going towards the Mevagissey Christmas Lights which is wonderful as they were beginning to get a bit tired. Even better Jetty Street is going to get some white ribbon lights and Christmas trees so it should look beautiful.

And it's not over yet we still have the Olympics to come as well as a few football matches which seem to be causing great excitement in the rest of the household. I'm a very fair weather football fan but if we get to the finals no doubt like the rest of the country I'll get excited and join in and if we win? I can't even begin to imagine how pleased that will make people. Oh and of course there's Wimbledon as well but I'm not putting any money on Murray but there I go being all pessimistic, far too British! I shall learn from our new found spirit of optimism and shout Come on Murray and then when he loses I shall grin ruefully and cross my fingers for next year, in true British style.

Never ever make reading a chore for children

I was on St Austell Bay Radio on Tuesday and had great fun, much less scary than I thought it was going to be but then I hadn't anticipated DJs on pogo boots, school kids and chocolate rolls.

I was in to talk about books for children which is trickier than you'd think. Too many children are put off reading at an early age because reading is made to be competitive due to the progressive reading schemes. The minute you make something competitive you have losers and there will be some children left behind. Children who get left behind end up disliking the activity.

First of all reading is a functional skill which takes us a while to get, for some of us it takes longer than others and the way we teach reading in this country means that for some children they will feel like failures as they fall behind their friends on the book schemes. If a child hasn't completely learnt to loathe books by the time they are functionally literate then the next hurdle is finding something they enjoy. There's a whole world of books out there and yet we seem to limit what kids can read to a narrow range of fictional titles.

We have an obsession with age specific reading (more pressure) and ditch picture books at the first opportunity because we think children are too old for them. I love Anthony Browne and Asterix and my childhood days are way behind me! If a child asks you to remove their picture books, box them up and "rediscover" them again a year later. They will leap on them with such enthusiasm. Picture books are fabulous, you can tell your own stories, there's different stuff for your brain to do, analysing images rather than processing text. Children should never be made to feel that picture books are for babies.

And it's not just picture books that get dismissed. Why isn't the Guinness Book of Records an acceptable reading book? Men tend to prefer non-fiction so maybe boys would prefer to read non-fiction as well? What about comics and graphic novels, they're telling stories, why aren't they considered acceptable?

All that we are left with is fiction but even then, that gets whittled down. We don't all like Fantasy so why on earth do we assume that all 11 year olds will love Harry Potter? Just because you liked Jane Austen as a girl why assume that your daughter will? And just because someone has decreed that Dickens is a classic it doesn't mean that they are right. Reading is about freedom, not coercion.

Having gone through all that, it's a wonder that anyone enjoys reading. There should be no pressure to read the popular title, or the approved title, or the hard book, or three books a week or to finish a book once you've started it. Just let kids pick up and put down books all day long, let them have a huge range of titles, don't test them on them and don't encourage them to read a certain amount. Just let them be and don't worry; if they're relaxed about reading and have access to books then one day something will click.

The fun you can have when you say yes!

Along with prevaricating less I have also felt that life might be more exciting if I said yes rather than no. Before I go further I'd like to state that my answer won't be yes to everything but just a bit more than I do now. Anyway, that's how I came to be driving over to Boconnoc Church in order to perform in a Scratch Messiah. In case you don't know what that means, and one week ago I was in your number, it means a last minute thrown together rehearsal and performance of Handel's Messiah. When my friends asked me, it sounded like a laugh, I used to be in a competition standard choir when I was younger and I thought I should be OK. At that point I was ignoring a few important facts, I had never sung the Messiah and it was a very long time ago since I was in a choir.

I was driving over to meet the girls on a gorgeous Saturday; issues of pee, poo, mud, rugby and boys were left behind and I raced through the autumn countryside humming away to the bits of the Messiah that I knew. Best just clarify that the boys were not responsible for the pee and poo issues. Neither was Steve. Agatha is still providing us with daily challenges but that's a whole other column.

Now where, was I? Ah yes, rolling through the Cornish countryside, trilling out my halleluiahs. Over the week I had managed to listen to the Messiah twice and I discovered that it was a lot longer than I realised, a lot more complicated and a hell of a lot higher than I could manage. Certainly I used to be a soprano but as I've got older I have found that my voice, along with other things, has started to head south. When I was singing top C it made the boys search for injured cats. My confidence was also beginning to head south.

I wasn't sure what to pack, so in went a skirt, heels, make up, scarf, hat, walking boots (churches aren't known for their heating) I also added some soup, rocky road, and apples and given the amount of pheasant on the lanes around Boconnoc I would soon also be packing a Game Pie.

Amid much nervous laughter the three of us arrived at the church to discover that we were late and we had to shuffle in and share scorebooks with other choristers. The plus sides were many; everyone else seemed to know roughly what they were doing, the Choir master was a forgiving man and the church had very efficient heating. The negatives however, were also many. The forgiving Choir master also assumed everyone got everything he said, after just one telling, the people around me may have known what they were doing but Jo, Rebecca and I were woefully adrift and the very efficient heating was beginning to make me sweat in my many layers. I was beginning to wonder why the hell I hadn't packed a bottle of water.

All too soon, and I really do mean too soon, the rehearsals were over and we were told to come back in an hour's time for the evening performance. The look of horror on Rebecca's face mirrored mine, surely that wasn't it? We didn't even know the words, let alone the tune, or the dynamics! Even so that was all the preparation that we were going to get.

As the moment approached a sense of dread and foreboding settled upon us, but we had forgotten just how good everyone around us was and of course given that it was a scratch performance how forgiving the audience were. It was a glorious evening and as I sang out to the skies, my voice soaring higher and higher I was thrilled that I had said yes.

80

St Austell needs another supermarket but where shall we put it?

Hands up who likes standing in queues, being barged by trolleys never finding anywhere to park and always trying to find where the sugar has been moved to. I don't see many hands up. So maybe we could do with another supermarket? We are the largest population centre in Cornwall so there are a fair few of us all using the two major supermarkets at any one time. When summer comes round and Cornwall swells up then trying to go shopping is an even worse nightmare, so I certainly think we could do with another supermarket and I have to say I'm pretty glad that it's Sainsburys; I just find its location a bit odd. Surely we have enough old industrial land to be able to house a shopping village the size of the one they're proposing rather than tearing up those lovely fields on the drive out of St Austell? I'm also not certain why anyone thinks the west of St Austell, where very few people live, is a good idea. To compound the issue they are going to build a Waitrose to the east of Truro, again on lovely rolling fields where no one lives. I'm really not sure how all the people traveling from Threemilestone across Truro or from Par along the bypass to get to these new supermarkets will help alleviate traffic congestion. In fact you'd be hard pressed to think of two worse bottle necks in Cornwall.

Clearly the planners are relying on the residents of the hugely under populated Roseland peninsular to plug the gap. Certainly many of the Roseland residents will appreciate having the choice of Waitrose and Sainsburys to go to but I think it's a bit much to expect them to support two massive hypermarkets. One can only buy so many pine nuts.

However, without being silly, St Austell does need more shopping opportunities if the council is to be able to raise revenue and they aren't going to be able to do that off the back of the White River Centre. Certainly things are beginning to get better but given its strange layout it was never going to be able to attract a department store and a good shopping centre needs a department store. Although I'm not impressed with the location, I think somewhere around Penwithick or Eden would make more sense, even par docks would be a good use of space, I do think we need the shopping village.

Like many of us I shop in Truro, online, Mevagissey and only very occasionally in St Austell but things are improving in the town. We just need a few more good places to eat, free parking and independent traders to make the place a second viable alternative to an out of centre shopping zone which is almost certainly going to happen no matter who protests. My first step to improve the town centre? Relocate the library into one of the shops. Bring in the Council offices and then you have more people about. Stop thinking of segregated shopping zones and start thinking about bringing things together. Oh and a tourist information centre in the town centre for heaven's sake. I wish people would stop telling me why it can't be done and start thinking about why it should be done. Right best stop before I start ranting but you know I'm right. Don't you?

My Olympic highlights

Whilst we wait for the Paralympics I wanted to share my favourite bits of the Olympics so far. It started in Bugle, as I'm sure many things do. I was driving through it about an hour before the flame was due to pass through and it seemed like the whole village was out. The village silver was proudly displayed on a table, brass bands were assembling in the side streets, bunting and flags festooned the road and every front door was open with people milling about, laughing and smiling. It was at this moment that I realised that we might be in for something very special for the next few months.

The momentum of the torch moved towards a parachuting Queen and a stunning opening ceremony with the most wonderful and artistic cauldron at the end.

I loved seeing the cheeky Czech delegates arriving in the Stadium in wellies! Even better was seeing women from countries that had never sent a woman before; even Saudi Arabia, who don't even let them drive, fielded female athletes. For Team GB our girls have been phenomenal, the first medals went to girls as did the last, the first gold went to a girl and in between they collected many more medals than ever before.

The technology in our stadiums was incredible, did you know the velodrome had been designed to be warmer than normal as warm air is slightly thinner and makes for faster cycling or that the baffles in the athletics arena were engineered to make it the loudest in the world?

Then there were the events themselves; the dead heat at the end of the female triathlon. Watching the Brownlee brothers coming first and third in their triathlon, the three Jamaican flags rising for the 200m and I really loved the expression on Katherine Copeland's face as she could not believe she had just won gold! Almost as good as Andy Murray's.

I was also so impressed with how the athletes celebrated with each other even when it meant they lost gold. In particular during the Men's High Bar final. Each time all the rivals clapped and hugged each other as stunning performance was followed by even more stunning performance. Those men were able to look at excellence and applaud it rather than show their own disappointment. I was touched by the tears from Pendleton when she saw her Gold changed to Silver but her huge smile and victory lap for the audience and her hug for her competitor were properly Olympian. As was the Jordanian, her face clearly in agony, but kept on to cross the line. There were times when getting a Bronze seemed even better than a Gold and it was a real laugh to see Tom Daly and his whole team jumping in the pool in celebration.

Even if I didn't get tickets I could still take part due to the wonderful BBC coverage and I'll never forget watching the diving on the shop computer with a German family, all rooting for each other's guy . Then there were the golden letterboxes – well done Royal Mail and finally sharing it all with my friends on Facebook who had been lucky enough to attend. All in all an outstanding affair.

How to improve British sports

I think it can be agreed that the Olympics has been a huge success but what has made it so successful? I would like to say that it's been a lot more than the amount of medals that we have won, although that has been great.

I believe there have been a range of reasons why it has been so successful, in the first place the whole thing worked. There were no gridlocks, no security scares, no unfinished buildings, all the scaremongering from the media came to nothing, we staged a welcoming, efficient, accessible set of games. The next reason was how we were able to follow every aspect of the games via the BBC. Their coverage has been exhaustive and we have all been able to follow whatever our particular interest is. We've also been able to watch sports that we never see on television; I never thought I'd get into watching Canoe sprints, dressage or BMX cross country. Since when was the long jump so exciting or the 800m so nerve wracking? I think this has been one of the keys to the sense of national pride; we have been able to join in and follow along. The next thing that has made it so successful has been how well the girls have done, gold after gold have fallen to our Amazons and they were so well deserved. Finally we have loved the tales of true grit; some of our athletes are headline acts that seem to do all right in terms of sponsorship but we've had people who have had to sleep on floors, kip in cars, sell stuff to fund their training. This seems to me to be the true Olympian spirit, these people are not in it for the money they just do it because they love it and they want to be the best. Here in Britain we love the underdogs and it seems that our underdogs have outperformed all expectations.

So where do we go from here? To me it seems obvious, show a wider range of sports on television, not just the paid channels. Support more female events, they outperformed the boys; let's see that excellence reflected on TV. BBC has an arts channel and a children's channel so why not a sports channel? Clearly some of us are interested in sports other than premiership football. Let's also get more money into grass root sports, help clubs, help parents with grants and get behind local events. Finally get games back into the school curriculum on a regular basis. Bring back competitive sports, they don't have to be all that is offered but children need to learn how to lose and how to cheer! Taught well, team sports can help children pull together. Even if you don't fancy team sports any sort of regular physical exertion is good for the body and good for the mind, *Mens sana in corpore sano!*

Of course the turn of the true Olympians come next with the Paralympics. The hype is probably going to be less intense than what we have seen over the past fortnight but what these competitors have overcome and will achieve will be no less stunning and probably more so!

Riptides and weaver fish – a memorable day at the seaside

Our first family day on the beach this year proved to be something of a disaster. My eldest had just bought his first surf board and had been desperate to take it out but we just hadn't been able to find the right day. Finally we found a day where, we were all at home, no one had any fixtures, the weather, whilst not sunny (ha ha), was also not foul and so we all piled into the car and headed to Gwithian. It was essential to me that we picked a beach with decent surf, never too busy and manned with lifeguards. As I don't surf, despite numerous attempts, Thomas was going to have to go in the surfing area on his own, body boarders have to stay in a different section of the beach for obvious safety reasons. However, he's only 13 and though he considers that fully grown, I don't, so no lifeguards, no surfing. He mucked around for about an hour coming to grips with his new board whilst we all body boarded nearby, after that he was exhausted and came to join us and Steve went back up the beach to read his book.

The weather as I said wasn't foul but it was incredibly windy, in fact the off shore breeze was so strong that every wave was plumed with a huge shower flying back into the faces of anyone on the wave behind so with big waves and a strong wind we were also getting quite tired. Thomas and I decided to have one last race in to join Finn at the beach and then we would go home. We were chatting and bobbing about waiting for the right wave when I looked up and was horrified to see how far the beach was! Seconds ago I had been able to stand up now I could barely pick Finn out. Thomas and I were amazed at the strength of the wind and started to paddle back in, to no avail. We tried again, nothing. I was now tired and beginning to get alarmed when I looked around to see a lifeguard swim up with her board. I have never been so damn relieved. She asked if we were OK and any notion of bravado went out the window. Thankfully as we were chatting a big set of waves came in and she asked if we would be able to catch them in, well I may have been knackered and worried but I could still catch a wave and Thomas and I rode it all the way into the shore, it was easily the best ride of the day. Back in the shallows the lifeguard who had ridden in with us came to double check on us and to explain what had happened. The wind had pushed us over in front of a rocky outcrop, when a rip developed and that was that. A rip! We were in the wrong place at the wrong time.

The bit that amazed me was that I know all about rips; I know how they form, where they form, how fast they move, how to avoid them and if caught in one, how to get out of them. Having never been in a rip tide though

I never realised what they felt like. They feel like nothing. I had always assumed you would feel a current or something. Had I been less tired I imagine that I would have put two and two together and paddled left or right to get out of the rip rather than towards the shore but I didn't.

We staggered up the beach happy that we have such a wonderful lifeguard network and better educated about what a rip tide feels like to discover Steve sitting in the lifeguard tower watching all the excitement whilst the lifeguards treated his weaver fish sting! Next time we're going rock pooling.

Walking the Saints Way with dogs, dragons and monsters

It's time again for the school's Saints' Way walk. Every year in the summer the school take the year six pupils on a trek across Cornwall, they stretch it out over three days and it gives the children a chance to get out of class. By the summer term they are ready to move on, they've done their SATs, sat their entrance exams, they can rings around the curriculum and they are itching to go up. Up to the big school with all the terrors and the excitements that it promises and suggests.

So in a rather smart move years ago it was decided to exhaust this over excited, nervous pack of puppies and the Saint's Way walk was born. Stage one is Fowey to No Man's Land above Lostwithiel, we were due to go two weeks ago but an early rain shower meant that it was called off despite howls of protests from the children and parents alike. Naturally the rest of the day proved dry and sunny. In fact it was probably the last dry and sunny day we've seen since. Yesterday we were scheduled to try again and as I woke up, I looked out the window to see heavy misty rain blowing along the street with almost no visibility and high winds. An even worse day than last time. However Mr F. was not to be thwarted a second time and the walk was on. The mini bus was loaded up with children, parents and dogs and we were off!

We jumped out at Fowey and stepped straight up to the church and the Saint's Way. Days out with Mr F. are always special because of the enthusiastic and bizarre way in which he presents information. Nothing in his mind is boring except maybe paperwork, no child is a failure so long as they are trying and very little is impossible. We started in the church where I discovered that during the civil war Cornish hospitality towards the Parliamentarians was lacking and they were all sent home naked having been beaten and had all their provisions removed. The pulpit is from the wrecked timbers of a Spanish galleon and that the decorative piece of stone in the graveyard came from atop of the church tower when it was struck by lightning.

We were about to set off on the Saints' Way but what exactly is it? This is an old path that connected the early Christian Celts in Ireland through Wales across Cornwall and down over to Brittany. As the saints and pilgrims progressed across the lands they were banishing the pagan religions as they went and brought the word of God to the people they met. So we were going to follow their route spreading the word of God banishing such pagan practices as worshiping water deities and woodland spirits. Looking around me I felt quite confident that the woodland nymphs and deities would be safe from our bunch of heathens!

Off we set, nattering and chattering, wrapped up against the wind and rain and soon we were walking up some very steep hills, shedding coats and jumpers as we went and very glad of the damp air to cool us down. Eventually we arrived at St Sampson's at Golant. A Holy Well stands at the entrance of the Church so maybe those water nymphs weren't so much banished as assimilated? Inside we discovered that St Sampson fought dragons and brought the dead back to life. Early saints seem to have more in common with super heroes rather than being nice, kindly folk. In an interesting aside Mr F suggested that dragons might have existed, in the form of fire breathing pterodactyls that ignited their own malodorous, methane burps with their rough teeth.

Who knows?

Saying yes lands me in deep water

Just got back from my first wind surfing lesson. I went out with Polkerris Watersports, a great crowd that have been teaching my boys to sail for the past few years so I had complete confidence in their teaching abilities and safety measures as well as in their friendliness. When you are about to make a complete wally of yourself it's good to know you won't be laughed at and that you won't drown. In that order.

It became quite clear early on, when I was the only one to fall off their board on dry land, that I wasn't a natural. The fact that I fell off a further two times should have given me some clues as to how the next three hours might progress. We were a small class of about seven plus two instructors, Adam in the safety boat and George out on a board with us. We practiced standing up, turning the board around and windsurfing all in the safety of the harbour. I soon realised that as hard as I had thought this might be I had under estimated it. At one point I fell off the board, fell into the water and was promptly rewarded with a crack on the side of my head via the mast. George quickly appeared alerted either by the sound of the thwack or the volume of my swearing or more likely because he was keeping a vigilant eye on all us novices. He duly explained that when you fall into the water to keep a hold of your mast as you will "instinctively" never let it come towards you and will push it away. So up I went again and given the amount of times I was falling in I was finding the getting up and balancing pretty easy.

It was just when I tried to do something with the sail that it all went horribly wrong. The next time I felt myself falling back I remembered George's advice and held onto the mast and promptly smacked it onto my head. I won't pretend it didn't hurt, it did, but it could have been worse. The fact that I was in water meant that at least my body, floating in water, was able to deflect the blow by sinking down. Now the problem was that I was drowning. I exaggerate but there I was bobbing under the sail, head throbbing and cursing like a banshee. Clambering back on board I checked to see if there was any blood and at this point any sane person would think well if it hurt that much maybe you should consider returning to the shore. But I'm either not that personality type or I'm a bloke so I persevered. Given that I also won't stop the car to ask for directions when I've temporarily misplaced my location (see, I can't even say lost) then maybe I am a bloke.

The limit was reached when I found myself constantly becalmed at one end of the bay, Adam assured me that I was just in a tricky wind spot, not actually useless and so I tugged my board to the other end of the bay, finally I seemed to have found the wind but also the waves and on one of my many falls my fingers got trapped between the mast and the board. Between the metal pole of the mast, the solid board and my fingers, only one of those was remotely pliable. Now I don't have great fingernails but they are at least pink, black is not a colour preference. I knew the game was up when I then started to kick my board and scream rude words at it. Whilst floundering in the surf. Once again, George to the rescue, who told me how one windsurfer had once punched a hole through his sail in frustration. I knew the feeling. Bruised, battered, exhausted but laughing I left the water and headed towards a hot chocolate along with the rest of the group. I'm undaunted though, I'll be back next week and maybe by week three I'll be able to stand up, travel in a straight line and then turn around again?!

Helping those who help themselves and helping those that can't

Something has been bothering me recently and has got me thinking about the phrase "help those that help themselves." I was listening to an article on Radio 4 about the state of the Spanish Banking system. The experts were saying that the Spanish banks were doing less to support their local economy than that of the Bank of England. His reasons for them doing less were partly that they were tied by the fact that they were part of the Euro and partly because they were expecting Brussels to sort things out. This rang huge bells with me, only the other week I had been chatting to Steve about overseas aid. There's another phrase that says "give a man a fish and he eats tonight, give a man a rod and he never has to ask for food again." The same maxim as helping those that help themselves.

It seems a strange phenomenon but the more you give people the less they seem to do for themselves, what you are doing when you take control is quite literally that. You TAKE control. You take power away from the people / institutions that you are trying to help. In taking the power away people seem to give up and throw off responsibility for the situation. There is an argument that says third world aid doesn't work, the Overseas Development Agency has lots of oddities to it. For example we give aid to India. Initially this seems OK to me when I think about the level of poverty in India but then I remember that they have a Space programme. If the Indian government has enough money for a space programme, which is no cheap venture, then maybe they should scrap it and look after their own people first.

I am absolutely not against helping those in need. I am proud that we are able to help countries that are struggling. Those that have had regions wiped out by natural disasters but I start to get twitchy when I see us sending money to countries that have enough money but choose not to spend it on their own people. If a country knows that every year it will receive X amount from other countries, it is viewed as income not aid. If the money was not forthcoming what would they do? I hate the thought that by withdrawing our money people would suffer but I would rather that we didn't waste our money.

The solution to me in these cases is trade rather than aid. Like it or loathe it a capitalistic infrastructure provides stability, if we were trading with countries in a fair manner we give them back the means of production and the ability to make their own money.

Regrettably I think the same thing happens much closer to home with our benefits system. Again I need to say that I am wholly in favour of benefits, I am more than happy that my money helps out those that can't help themselves, I would even be prepared to pay more because I hate to think of the elderly and the disabled struggling, or mothers unable to feed their children, all these people I want to help. I just don't want to help those that choose not to work. Given that we have over two million unemployed I wonder what jobs are found by all the foreigners that come over here to work? Of course there are good and genuine reasons why some people can't work, what we need to do is make sure that we are not propping up those that find work a chore.

Take it on the chin and fail

You can tell that the summer term is almost over as the school sports day arrives. Incredibly we have never once had a rainy sports day, what are the odds of that? Once again we arrived at Par track to watch our children giving their all, whilst we munched on strawberries being sold as a school fundraiser. We have some very enterprising people on our PTA, I headed straight for the Pimms' canopy only to discover that what they were selling may well have been fruity but it wasn't intoxicating. Lured under false pretences – very clever! Sports day is one of those gorgeous moments in the school calendar where parents can lean over the rails and shout out encouragements and praise each other's children and beam inwardly when their own children do well. It's even nicer to see the whole school running along the last runner to encourage them over the finishing line.

How very different in secondary school or rather I wouldn't know if it was different as parents aren't invited. I don't know if that's a school thing or a pupil thing but I think it's a damn shame. To make matters worse my eldest doesn't even know if he has won anything. He came first in some heats but then they didn't do a heats final so presumably it's down to the fastest time and furthest jump / throw. His sports day was two days ago, maybe he'll find out in assembly tomorrow? Year seven can be so difficult for children. They don't know the routines of the new school and they've gone from being the top of the school, to being an afterthought, right back at the beginning again. It's also another example of how the role of the parent gets pushed back. I know parents need to start giving their older children more space but as children hit their teens and start to take exams, they need more parental support not less, albeit in a more background capacity.

So, do I have an Olympic athlete on my hands, who knows? Well, I do, and the answer's I think not but I would have liked to have gone to the Olympics with the boys next year just to see and take part. However, I'm afraid that the whole application business left me in the dark. I went through various application forms and then had to make a stab at what I would like to see. Having entered all the events I was interested in I discovered I had committed over £3000. Eek. What if I got them all? How to give my bank manager a heart attack in one quick move. The more I thought about it the more I realised it was a nonsense. "What if I successfully got tickets for Day Two and Day Ten? Do I travel to London twice? Where do I stay? Do I want to watch the sailing at Weymouth, what will I actually see? Can I really justify the expense of the Opening Ceremony?" In the end I gave up. Apparently on some European

110

sites you can simply buy the tickets for the events you want   without this bizarre pot luck approach that we seem to have opted for and if that fails then next year I'm going to take the boys back to Par Track, get some gold chocolate coins and host my own Olympics, where the boys will of course win everything!

Fudge failures and the Royal Cornwall Show

I know the Royal Cornwall Show is a fabulous occasion, I know it brings people together, I know it is a time when the county shows off its finest but for me it's a time of dread. Each year, it looms over me until the awful letter comes home from school, the one inviting the children to take part in the honey cookery competition. Every year, the school invites the children to take part and every year the children choose to make the fudge. I could scream! I hate the honey fudge recipe. The children have taken to picking fudge, I am sure, just to see my reaction. Now I know the purist (and the judges) amongst you will be exclaiming, "Surely, the children do the cooking?!" but if you think I'm letting primary school children boil and pour molten sugar you've got a screw loose. So what we will do this year will be what we have done every year; the boys will read the recipe, gather and measure the ingredients, tip them in and stir until it starts to heat up. At this point I will step in and ruin it. Every year I step in and ruin it. I don't know how but each and every time something different occurs. Over the years, the boys have handed in black fudge, brittle fudge, fudge that couldn't be broken with a toffee hammer, fudge that melted off the presentation plate and so on and these would be the second or third attempts.

The boys love it, they get to eat the first failures and then proudly take in the mess that I have made of their cooking. As you might have guessed they have yet to win anything for fudge in five years. I should imagine that the judges look at the two plates of the sorriest looking fudge on record and comment that here are entries unsullied by the help of any adult. It would be funnier if it wasn't so mortifying, I'm normally a decent cook but honey fudge is clearly my nemesis When it is the youngest boy's final year I'm going to the fudge shop in Mevagissey and getting their finest honey fudge and putting it on a plate!

Thankfully the boys don't have the hindrance of their mother for the other entries and have great fun making the school scarecrow, planting up flowers in unusual containers, making insect masks and various other entries. I love walking around the competition tents on the show day to see all the various entries. If you've not popped into that tent before it's really worth the time to see what the local schools have been up to. My one regret is that it only seems to be a handful of schools that take part each year. I understand the constraints on the time and resources of schools but a county show is a wonderful occasion for us all to see what each of us has been getting up to. If you do look in though please walk past the honey fudge table quickly.

I don't like "emmets"

Saw my first feathered swallows this week and it was wonderful. Given the great weather we've been having I wouldn't be surprised if they've been around longer but if they have I've not been observant enough. In Tenerife, when the summer ends and the winter tourists and holidaymakers arrive they call them "swallows" in common with the birds they are leaving the cold northern shores for warmer climes. It's said with fondness and not a little bit of smugness, those on the island revel in the fact that their island is so loved that people flock to it all year around supporting their economy long into the winter months.

How much nicer a description than "emmet." It's said that when the Tamar Bridge first opened someone quipped that as the line of traffic crawled across, they looked like emmets – the Cornish word for ants. I can't find anything to back this up though; the other suggestion is that the holiday makers swarm around on the beaches getting redder and redder, again like ants. Still I suppose "ants" does make sense, what I think doesn't make sense is the snide, sneery way that it is said. Maybe some say the word with kindness but I've never heard it used nicely. Now I'll put my hands up here and confess that I am not Cornish – and as I've only been here 12 years I'm still classed as an "incomer" another friendly welcoming term but my children are born here so maybe there'll be hope for us in a century or two.

The point is that I've never been made to feel unwelcome; I find Cornwall a very friendly and open county. When I meet people for the first time I don't check out their lineage and they don't check out mine, we meet as equal strangers and we either like each other or not. It's never based on where our grandparents are buried. So I find it disheartening to hear people being called emmets or bloody emmets or worse. Of course it's maddening when they get in the wrong lane on the mini roundabout but who ever heard of a three lane mini roundabout anyway? And yes I know it's enough to make you weep when you are bonnet to bonnet with a car pulling a caravan along a lane but I bet they're weeping more.

I've met as many rude Cornish as I have visitors and the fact that some use the word "emmet" in a derogatory fashion proves the point. We live in a great county no wonder people want to visit or live here who can blame them, they come and bring their hard earned money which I for one am rather glad to see, as are a great many other businesses in the county.

I like Mrs Doasyouwouldbedoneby, be nice to people and most of them will be nice back, call them names, belittle them and sneer at them and they may well do the same back. Now I'm back off out to enjoy this glorious weather, I hope when you read this it's still good.

Saying one thing, meaning another

Steve was looking at an old Zippo the other day and commented on their Lifetime Guarantee, he thought it was a pretty impressive testament to the belief in their product that Zippo were prepared to offer such a guarantee. Now it could be that I'm a picky old soul but to me their offer was good but it was only a lifetime guarantee for the life of their business not of the purchaser's. Were they seriously suggesting that if Zippo went bust that they had insurance policies in place so that 50 years later a customer could get their money back if the lighter failed. Even if the company had gone bust 30 years previously? It's just not realistic is it? So a lifetime guarantee sounds good but it's not your lifetime, it's theirs.

That's the whole thing about adverts and advertisers, they are wonderful wordsmiths, the English language is their bread and butter and every single word they use has been thought about. I remember ASDA used to put on the back of their shampoo bottle "ASDA is against animal testing" Now again I'm being picky but that does not say "This product was not tested on animals" So my thoughts were that the majority of their products were not tested on animals as a preference but that some were. This meant that they could state a positive message but not be held accountable for it. Am I being too cynical? I just think a corporate giant like Wal-Mart knows exactly what it means when it says something and so do its lawyers.

I don't think advertising and product promotion is a bunch of outright lies but I do think it is all about smoke and mirrors and sleight of hand.

There's an advert on at the moment for a roll-on waxing product that claims eight out of ten women who used it would use it again. Sounds good but when would they use it again? Next month? If they were desperate? If they were paid? What's the pain threshold of these women? The selling points of the product are that it doesn't burn you and it doesn't leave a mess. To be fair when looking at a hair removal product these aren't high on my selling points. I'd be looking for pain free and for length of grow back time. The fact that it won't burn me sounds like a plus point but it also won't electrocute me, or run me over. So they are selling me a concept that isn't even an issue and making it sound like a positive.

What these adverts are doing are using "weasel words" a phrase coined to mean an empty statement. For example; children who eat Nutella have more energy during the day. (Compared to children that had nothing at all for breakfast) eight out of ten people agree with reduced jail sentences (those questioned were currently in jail) "It has been shown that…" Really? Where has it been shown? Or how about, "The majority of people think" Prove it! Using "the majority" suggests that if you aren't part of the club you are out of step and therefore wrong. And even if a majority does think something it doesn't mean that they are right.

Next time you watch the ads listen out for the weasel words. Oh and I believe the politicians may use them from time to time as well.

A rant on rude visitors

This is aimed at a tiny, tiny minority but I'm so riled right now by the holidaymaker who has just shouted at me that I had to scribble out my fury. By and large people are lovely but some people are just rude and this goes out to them. Sleeves rolled up, here we go. We are not slow or stupid down here and we do speak English so there's no need to sneer at us or speak loudly or slowly. If we're looking dumbfounded it may simply be down to the shock at hearing such ridiculous or offensive statements.

If you can't reverse your car please consider if you should be driving? Please don't sit and stare at me and wave me imperiously back. You have a passing space three meters behind you, mine is half a mile back. I know this because I live here, I'm not being mean or difficult but all you have to do is reverse your car three meters. And please don't shout at me. I know my car is shabby and dirty and yours is huge and shiny but when I pull over to let you pass, would you also mind moving over? I know the lane is narrow and bordered by stone and thorns but unless we both squeeze in we won't pass each other.

Incidentally, if you're towing a caravan or driving a campervan please don't take the interesting shortcut. Please. Cornish lanes are rubbish for anything larger than a car, they narrow down in the blink of an eye and all signs instantly disappear, no junction or cross road is going to give you a clue. Oh and don't rely on your sat nav, because if it's wrong it's a right struggle to reverse two miles uphill.

Yes, the parking is expensive but we have to pay it as well – all year, not just for the week. Mevagissey is a village, how many of your villages have free cash points. It's not my fault that you have no mobile phone reception; I have, so it's not because we're in the back of beyond but rather because your network provider is pants.

We are a historic fishing village, the cobbles stay. The width of the roads are pretty much determined by the houses so I'm sorry but we can't add pavements. We don't mean to make it a "death-trap" but we're not going to close the village to traffic, we live and work here, we have to get in and out. I know that the roads are only one car wide but we are still two-way on all the roads, yes I know that can make life tricky but there we go.

This is a bookshop not a crèche, at 6pm I do not expect you to leave your son in here reading whilst you go for a pint next door. Speaking of food and drink, don't bring it in here, I can't sell books covered in ice-cream and don't sneer at me when I asked you in a really friendly

126

voice to put the pasty away, I know your dog can clean up the bits of potato that you've dropped but that's not really the point is it?

To everyone else, you're lovely; you come in here with such enthusiasm and smiles. Your children are curious, interesting and well mannered, you are engaging and we see you season after season and you make working in the shop great fun. You come back with tales and laughs and make my day.

Thanks for letting me rant. Rabbit pie next week!

Farewell little school

Well, here we are, July and a milestone in our lives, our eldest boy is leaving primary school. How did this happen? Where did the time go? It really did seem like just the other day when he first toddled into school looking ludicrously cute in his tie and blazer. I remember looking at the tall, confident scruffy Year Six boys and wondered what it would be like, to be the mother of such a grown up child. Five years on and I look at my tall, confident scruffy boy and realise that he is still five in my heart and probably always will be, no matter how much he hates it!

On the school run this morning I had three 11 years olds all saying their favourite word. We had a five minute recital of Bum, Freak and Wag where they sounded like the frogs' chorus with my nine year old laughing his head off. They then launched into Postman Pat and promptly forgot the words. It was a fun trip and I was thinking how much they enjoyed going to school, I don't remember much laughter when I used to go to school. Surely the mark of a good primary school is not where it sits in league tables but where it sits in a child's heart?

Over the years the boys have learnt to sail, surf and swim, played in football matches and run cross country for their school. They've walked the Saints Way from south to north coast and run miles for Sports Relief, they've cooked for the Royal Cornwall Show, taken part in concerts and hosted radio shows. In amongst all of this they've also learned to read, write and count to a squillion. As parents we've joined the children on bike rides, trips to the Minack, humiliated ourselves in the parents' swim race and joined in the family feel of the school. That is what a good school should be, part of an extended family. It should be a place where a child runs in every day laughing, where they discover teachers that they will remember for the rest of their lives, where they try as hard as they can because they want to not because they have to. I'll confess at this point that my children aren't always that motivated, before any teachers reading this choke with laughter or disbelief. Like any family there are going to be grumpy days as well as good ones.

Too often schools seem to be criticised for failing to gain suitable SAT levels, teachers are deemed unsatisfactory if their paperwork isn't properly presented. Head's are stressed by the amount of hoops the have to jump through, introducing initiative after initiative whilst wondering where the money is going to come from. But surely primary school should just be about developing a child's love of learning, keeping children safe and happy. Secondary school is going to be tough enough without children already arriving disenchanted. When I worked at Newquay Tretherras I saw such world weary, fed up children arrive in year seven and I would wonder how rotten their primary years must have been. So thank you to all the teachers out there, that love and care for your pupils, who know that a happy, motivated child is more important than SAT levels and attendance figures. I'm glad that you are in the majority and I hope that you all enjoy your holidays. On a personal note, thank you to all at Roselyon for helping transform my stumbling toddler into a confident, happy young lad.

This time saying yes lands me in shallow water

If there's one job I wouldn't thank you for right now it's being a goal keeper, not that anyone's asked me, mind. It seems that for 90 minutes or even longer you successfully stop all goals, for two seconds you let one go in and you're Judas. Suddenly everyone in the country has an opinion and the belief that even they could have stopped that one. It amazes me that we do so poorly for goalies in this country because apparently there seem to be enough experts around who could do a better job, including my nine year old son, the barmaid, my brother in law and of course my husband. Incidentally my husband could also play forward or on the wing. In fact if Mr Capello just contacted Steve and asked him to step up I'm sure he could win the match single handed.

Now this might sound like a girlie moan about football but I actually enjoy the World Cup, it's a time when the whole world seems to be focused on the same thing. If you type in World Cup on Twitter you are engulfed with strands of text in every language and alphabet possible. It's wonderful, so many people are happy and desperately focused on hoping that their country succeeds. As countries are knocked out teams develop new fans, suddenly we're all backing Ghana.

I'll watch the odd match and enjoy it but I'd rather be doing than watching so when I was offered the chance to have a yoga and surf lesson a few weeks ago I jumped at it. The session was being organised by Catch A Wave CIC They believe that surfing should be enjoyed by everyone, not just young gods and goddesses. Now I'm not saying that I am not a goddess but I'm a goddess that's a bit lumpy and achy and not quite as young as I once was.

We started with a yoga session and stood on the sand and stretched and loosened our bodies until they were wonderfully long and supple. We were tall, majestic and glorious. Then we ran down to the waves where we got pummelled and rolled and looked like flotsam that the sea had spat out.

Surfing for me was a bit of a hit and miss affair; the simple advice was grab your board, jump up, stick your butt out and crouch like you're going to the loo in France. Now due to my basic anatomical structure, sticking my posterior out was not a problem and having frequented French roadside lavatorial facilities I have no problems with crouching but "jump up"?! There were some serious gravitational issues to be overcome and I have to confess I had limited success. I really tried to stand up but it seemed that every time I got up, the momentum carried me forwards and I'd run off the front; again and again and again.

Even though I was rubbish and didn't have the strength, agility or fitness to actually ride a wave standing, I had a blast. And despite the amount of times I wiped out in spectacular fashions I honestly didn't ache the following day and I put that down solely to the preceding yoga session. This is their whole ethos, life should be fun for everyone no matter how infirm and the sea is a free and fabulous resource available to all. Nothing is as much fun as screaming down the face of a wave even if it's just lying on your tummy. I was reminded of how inclusive surfing can be the following day at the beach when two ladies who were easily in their 70s, walked out of the waves, one was in a cossie carrying a state of the art boogie board, the other was in a state of the art wetsuit carrying one of the old wooden belly boards. Both ladies were grinning ear to ear.

I wish Catch a Wave every success, incidentally, Steve doesn't surf but if he did I'm sure he be an expert at that too!

When it comes to childcare we are all in it together

What's that sound? Or rather what's that lack of sound? Oh no hang on, I can hear something, there in the background – it's the collective sigh of thousands of parents as their children go back to school. But there's also another sigh of relief, this time from the bosses and colleagues that have to try to cope with the pressures that the school holidays bring. It's easy to think that school holidays only affect families but of course they affect everyone. For two concentrated months it seems that half the British workforce needs to take time off, either to go on holiday or to provide childcare. It would help if schools were more flexible about family holidays. I do understand that six weeks is a great big holiday but it's also the most expensive time to do it and it's also the busiest time to do it and it puts the whole country under an enormous strain.

It's a strange position to be in as a parent but I often think that parents are guilty of forgetting that our child free colleagues are also in it with us. When three people in the department all have to take their holiday in August then you can bet that the fourth person without children will come fourth in the list of priorities, and of course poor old number four will also have to work extra hard in August acting as lynch pin and co-ordinator whilst the rest of the team are having fun in far flung exotic locations. Of course they probably aren't having fun; they are probably sun burnt and wondering how they are going to pay for the holiday that would have been £1500 cheaper just three weeks later. Still if you're stuck filing in back home with an increasing backlog then you won't be seeing it from their point of view.

Some parents seem to feel that because they have children then their needs must be met first. I've had to stop myself laughing when I once heard a serious argument that society owed parents because parents were continuing the species. Now that's probably the most self-serving argument I have ever heard. I didn't have children in order to honour my Darwinian debt and if I did, it was done subconsciously. I did it because I wanted children, so no one owes me anything. My children are my luxury and my gift, they are not my meal ticket or my excuse to push to the front of the queue. I am really grateful for everyone who helps me, and acknowledges that having children is hard work and does things to make life easier for me, but I don't expect it. Human kindness usually ensures that those with children never have to work the Christmas Eve shift if it can be avoided but it's not a given.

Unfortunately having children does mean that as parents we make them our first priority which is as it should be but it also puts a huge pressure on industry. In the past men worked and women stayed at home and ran things from there but we no longer live in that society, as mothers also work to make ends meet and childcare is increasingly spread over two parents. Gradually, what is actually happening is that childcare is spread out over everyone's shoulders, whether they have children or not. If a parent has to drop out of work to nurse a sick child the rest of the workforce picks up the slack. It may not seem like Cameron's Big Society but in a small way we're already all pulling together everyday. We just need to acknowledge it and realise that no one has the soft option on the holiday rota.

The Glories of October

I had a lovely walk into the shop this morning. I often park out on the harbour wall and walk in; it gives me time just to enjoy the peace and silence. It was a gorgeous, sunny day with hardly any breeze but there must be quite a swell out in the Atlantic somewhere because the waves would suddenly surge up and slap against the wall followed by a small shower of water on the road. Looking over the harbour it looks like the old lifeboat place is nearly finished. Those flats are going to have stunning views but the windows look a bit stingy and it's a shame the final finish is so, well, dull. It's some sort of stone or brick that doesn't look like any other building over on that side. What was wrong with render painted in a nice bright colour? Or slate hung? Or wildly modern with loads of glass? Still if anyone wants to offer me one, I'd not turn it down.

As I came around the harbour wall the fishermen were all shouting back and forth sorting out nets and catching up on the news. One bloke seeing an old mate shouted out "Hey Bob, thought you'd died!" Bob turned round and said "Nah, too busy for that!"

I have always thought that October is a gift to the residents of Cornwall. The sea is warm and when it's sunny the air is still warm enough to go and laze on an empty beach. The roads are clear again and we can amble to our destination, not tear and race and vent our frustrations on all and sundry. There are still lots of visitors around but they seem to have fallen into the same relaxed pace that we're all feeling and as there are visitors here, those of us who rely on the tourist trade aren't yet panicking. The heady days of August when the till didn't stop ringing are behind us but there's still money coming in, it's not as much but it will do.

The weather has also been glorious as it so often is in October and I've been discovering some lovely new walks, there's a great one along the river at Lerryn and another fabulous one heading from Melinsey Mill to Pendower Beach. The countryside is rich with pickings right now and I found a wonderful clump of penny buns the other day – very tasty mushrooms and I'm having them with rabbit tonight (thanks Dave!). The sloes are fattening up nicely so that will be Sloe Vodka for Christmas and I'm eyeing up the local geese which are also fattening up nicely.

For families the ordeal of September has now passed; the children have finally worked out where double ICT is and have finally accepted that homework is a necessary evil. The school run has settled down and everyone knows where they are to be picked up, dropped off, who has what bags and what homework has to be handed in the following day.

And of course October always ends with parties, Halloween and Guy Fawkes Night (I know not strictly October – but October's an embracing month, so the more the merrier). It's a great opportunity to stand all wrapped up against the elements and look up at the stars, the fireworks and the odd passing witch.

So I love October, the start of log fires, warm days and chilly nights, red leaves, quiet beaches and a sense of calm and relaxation. I hope you're all having an equally good month.

The Joy of Science

There's something geeky about loving science which I've never understood, probably because I love science but I can't understand why it doesn't fascinate everybody. You don't have to like all aspects of science but it's such an enormous field that there is bound to be something that appeals to everyone. It's such a fun area where you can question and challenge and experiment forever. I like to think about the human body. I mean why are we built the way we are? We really are very badly designed. Our nice, strong hard bones are on the inside surrounded by soft vulnerable bits. Ask any crab or lobster or tank designer and they'll agree that the hard protective case goes on the outside. Then there are our fun bits, situated within millimetres of our waste disposal area. Not the most harmonious of neighbours, just imagine... no, actually, don't do that, not pleasant.

Then there's our command centre, our brain, the bit that makes us unique and keeps us going. Is it protected, safe and unassailable? No. It swings around like any other appendage; the problem is that whilst we can carry on if a leg of an arm gets chopped off, without our head the show is over. Even worse, the unprotected narrow column that attaches it to our body also houses our main artery and windpipe. Any major damage to the neck that supplies our next two most essential items, the lungs and heart and once again it's goodnight Vienna. Having the brain behind a skull and lungs and heart behind ribs is not much cop when the neck is left so exposed. Another design oversight.

The best thing about science and the "what if" world is that I can read about it all day long in science fiction. For centuries authors have been finding the novel a perfect arena to test ideas and concepts. Gulliver's Travels, War of the Worlds, Frankenstein, The Time Machine these are all science novels and of course today there are hundreds of writers in the field; some of my favourites are Iain M Banks, Alastair Reynolds, Charles Stross, Isaac Asimov or for humour I love Terry Pratchett and Jasper Fforde. This passage comes from the mouth of a dragon in "The Last Dragonslayer" by *Jasper Fforde.*

"Only seeing the visible spectrum is like listening to a symphony and hearing only the kettle drums. Let me describe what I can see: at the slow end of the spectrum lie the languorous long radio waves that move like cold serpents. Next are the bright blasts of medium and short radio waves that occasionally burst from the sun. I can see the pulse of radar that arrears over the hills like the beam of a lighthouse and I can see the strange point-sources of your mobile phones, like raindrops striking a pond. I can see the buzz of microwaves and the strange thermal images of the low infrared. Beyond this is the visible spectrum that we share; then we are off again, past blue and out beyond violet to the ultraviolet. We go past google rays and manta rays and then shorter still to the curious world of the x-ray, where everything bar the most dense

146

materials are transparent...I can see all this, a beautiful and radiant world quite outside your understanding."

Isn't that great? I wonder if we would take better care of our planet if we could see it better? In some parts of the country there's a club called Café Scientifique where they hold monthly talks in wine bars and coffee house. Maybe the Eden Project or Heligan would like to set one up? Would I be the only one there?

Walks with Harry

We've been having some really beautiful weather recently. I appreciate that having typed this, it will now start to rain and by the time you read this you will no doubt be up to your armpits in water and beginning to develop webbed feet. If this is the case then I apologise whole heartedly. But for now, the good weather has meant that my walks with my constant companion, Harry, have been enjoyable experiences. Actually "constant" isn't a terribly good descriptive word for a companion who is by my side for about 10 seconds during the whole walk, but he does nip back now and then to check up on my laborious progress or to show me a rabbit that he has managed to catch, or even better a rabbit that someone else caught a week ago. Dogs do love a good strong smell and in his generosity, Harry assumes that I do too.

For this reason my preferred walks with Harry don't end near a rabbit warren. Too many times I have made the mistake of not getting him back on the lead in time and then just waiting uselessly whilst my dog undergoes paroxysms of ecstasy as he dashes uselessly from one thicket to the next. I also like to end the walk near a source of running water, this means that he can have a drink and I can give him a quick scrub down because the thing that Harry loves almost as much as a good scent is a good mud pool. In fact if he can find a stagnant bog then he is in heaven. It always amazes me how even in the most severe of droughts my oh so white dog can find the last patch of dark, stinking mud available.

It is fun watching him play though, he'll go from walking to trotting, then a wee bit of a jog and suddenly he'll see a movement and he accelerates from a canter to a gallop to finally flying as he launches himself through the scrub and up and over obstacles with his back legs flicking out behind him. Despite these Nimrod like qualities he just about always fails and pads back to me, tongue lolling, having enjoyed the chase as much as any end goal.

Walks on the beach are just as much fun, all those wonderful seagulls which hang teasingly above his head. The other day he was so intent on launching himself at a flock of seagulls that he completely misjudged the depth of water beneath his pads and suddenly plunged into a deeper section and had to doggy paddle his way back to a shallower point. As I watched the seagulls laugh at him I thought about the best way to describe the shock on his face for this column and to comment on how rather vacant in the brain department my dog is, when my foot plunged into a hidden dip in the icy cold sea and water poured down the top of my boot. I don't know if I actually heard Harry snigger but his tongue was definitely lolling in an even more laughing fashion than normal. As I sloshed back to the car I decided not to comment on the intelligence of anyone who fails to spot dips on the seabed.

What Scottish 16 year olds can teach us

Chilly nights and the new Bond film have set me thinking of Scotland again but even without these prompts, Scotland is very much on my mind at the moment due to the upcoming referendum. Will Scotland choose to leave the United Kingdom? An issue that is going to cause a lot of talk and speculation but hopefully no change. An aspect that I am finding really fascinating about the whole debate though is that the vote is being opened up to 16 and 17 year olds. This decision, I think, will have far greater ramifications. Thin end of the wedge, horse has bolted, genii is out of the bottle; however you phrase it, once you say that Scottish 16 years can vote on a national topic then why can't all 16 year olds vote in national elections? Or any elections?

I was chatting to a father the other day who felt it was a really bad idea as children will just vote the way their parents tell them. Interesting to hear that argument being used again, I think it was last dusted off during the time of the suffragettes, and before that, letting servants vote and so on. Personally, I think if you tell the majority of teenagers to do one thing you can be sure they'll do the exact opposite. Besides, once they are in the polling booth no one knows how any one has voted.

Certainly many teens will not bother to vote but when we have a national voters turn out, of under 60% I don't think the adult population has anything to boast about. A 16 year old can live independently, work full time, have children, get married. They are legally responsible for themselves and can make their own medical decisions and be responsible in a court of law. They can even join the army with their parents' consent. And yet they can't vote. Surely every aspect of their lives is affected by the decisions made by government but they have no say. For example, on the minimum wage tariff, anyone under 18 earns £3.68 an hour; someone over 21 earns £6.19 for the exact same job. Hardly fair. Maybe something they might like to vote on?

Of course the government passes laws that affect the rights of children; they don't get a vote because they are children and because they are still in the care of adults. Whilst the vast majority of 16 – 17 year olds are still at home with their family, they are now legally on a different footing and if they can be held responsible in law and pay taxes towards the government through their earnings then I believe that they have the right to vote.

Personally I think that they'll shake things up a bit. They're all wide eyed and enthusiastic, they get worked up about stuff, they fight and argue all the time, they are passionate and they care. If politicians think that they won't understand the issues then the politicians had better earn their wages and explain the situation properly. If the current voters are concerned that a youth vote may unsettle the apple cart then maybe they had better get off their apathetic behinds and vote. What I'm looking forward to is a pincer movement from the retired voters and the teenage voters and maybe we'll get a new political party that's in in for the people rather than themselves?

Giddy stuff, this Scottish air!

Game pie and free food

Ranting over, rabbits ready! Before I moved to Cornwall I had a rather romantic view of the huntin', shootin' fishin' chaps. In my mind they would be togged in tweed and deer stalkers, guns resting in the crook of their arms as they strode across the heather with Loch Lomond below them and the highlands rising above.

What I wasn't expecting was Warren. Towering above six foot with extra inches added by his dark black spiked up hair dressed in leathers, sporting a skateboard in one hand, a jackdaw in the other and an accent so broad he could skate across it if he choose. He wandered into the bookshop one day and we got chatting, as you would do with anyone whose companion is a live jackdaw – they have beautiful blue eyes!

Anyway it turned out that Warren would go shoot bunnies of an evening and I said I hadn't had rabbit in yonks and one thing lead to another and the following day in wandered Warren with two rabbits. Two rabbits still very much as nature had intended, guts and gizzards and fur and dull, life deprived eyes. I guess I must have looked horrified as Warren asked if I didn't know how to dress them. Oh they were so soft and fluffy, the idea of taking a knife to them made me feel pathetic. Warren took instant pity, swept the rabbits up again and said he'd be back shortly. Two hours later there were my rabbits all dressed and looking far more like dinner and less like Peter Rabbit. For the rest of the day they sat in a plastic bag by my feet, we didn't have the luxury of a fridge, with me wondering how high rabbit meat could get before it was no longer fit to eat.

From rabbit we went onto pigeon and even gave squirrel a try. I am such a carnivore I'll give anything a go but, my word, squirrel was a revelation. Really sweet and gamey – nothing like chicken.

Since then we have been the very lucky recipients of gifts from the field and sea. We have received fish and game in exchange for money, in exchange for books and sometimes we are the grateful recipients of gluts and freezer clear-outs.

Moving to Mevagissey we have been showered with further treats, mackerels are an unsurprisingly common offering. We've had them soused, stuffed and smoked. We even had a turbot in return for some books and it turns out that Dave goes shooting so now we've got rabbits, quail, pheasant, pigeon and partridge filling the freezer. Well they never make it to the freezer to be honest. In fact Dave gave me a whole bunch of goodies from his freezer once which I put in the back of my car and promptly forgot about. Oh the smell! The meat was good but the blood drained all over the boot. Harry was like a dog with ten tails.

Best recipe for rabbit at the moment is as follows. Grab a big casserole pan. Chop some onions into chunky bits with some garlic and fry in olive oil, then chop your rabbit into quarters, coat it in seasoned flour and then brown it off in the pan. Chop up some chorizo and throw that into the pan, pop in a couple of red peppers, cut nice and chunky. Add water, wine and some tins of tomatoes plus whatever herbs you have lying around, marjoram, oregano, thyme. You want the rabbit to be covered in liquid. Put a lid on the casserole pot and simmer for ages (hour minimum) either in an oven or on a stove; just before you're ready to eat also throw in mussels, cockles, clams whatever's to hand. It's easy to do, one you can walk away from and tastes gorgeous. Eat with some lovely fresh bread to dip in the sauce.

What did I want to be when I grew up

Being a barrister seemed to be on the cards for a while, it turned out that people would pay me a lot of money to be an argumentative, smart arse and my grandfather was a Judge so it seemed like a logical choice. However, a marine archaeologist seemed more glamorous, it would be really cool to discover Atlantis and lots of sunken gold. I then moved on to travel and figured foreign correspondent / photographer was where my calling was. Just so long as I had regular running water and room service. So it came as a shock to me when I had my interview with my career's advisor to discover that I was apparently best suited to being a hairdresser on a cruise liner. Anyone who has ever met me knows I don't care too much about my own appearance let alone anyone else's and as for making small talk with strangers that's a no-no, an even bigger no-no is being stuck with a bunch of strangers that I can't get away from so the cruise liner idea is my idea of hell.

Now, the same ridiculous questions are being posed to my eldest, the best I can say to him are that his GCSEs will not set him up for life, they will not shape the rest of his existence and that he is not to freak out if he chooses the wrong options. There's just so much more pressure for him than there was for me, nowadays he has to get at least 30 A levels, they must all be A stars and he must then go to University and accrue more debt that he can contemplate, if his life is to mean anything. And he's only 12.

Of course a good education is important but it's not essential that you know what you are going to do when you grow up. I mean which of us is actually doing the job we wanted when we were 12? I'll bet it's only a tiny handful. There just aren't enough train driver jobs to go around anyway. Then of course these days no one is in a job for life, unless he goes into one of the professions, so he's bound to jump around a bit.

Last year he was going to be an outdoors instructor. He's a bit of an adrenaline junkie so I can see the appeal but he got it into his head that he can earn £40K a year doing that and I'm not so sure. Then he decided that being an architect was the way to go, however he thinks the Royal Albert Hall would look better with a smooth white render finish to "bring it up to date" so I hope for the sake of this country's heritage that he doesn't pursue that career path. His most recent decision has brought me out in a cold sweat. He wants to join the army, maybe the paras, maybe an officer. I am very calmly nodding and saying the right things whilst inwardly swearing that if I ever lay my hands on Bear Grylls it may be an encounter that he fails to survive.

For what it's worth I became a librarian, didn't see that coming; a mother, really didn't see that coming and then started my own business. Being in charge, surrounded by books? I think my family saw that   coming from a very early age. Whatever children grow up to be, the important thing is that they have the   opportunities to experiment, change their minds, jump tracks and never ever listen to their careers advisor!

Words fail me

There are times when I find that there are not enough words in the human language to explain my situation and on other occasions I simply don't have the vocabulary. The other week I found myself trying to think how to explain to Trevor what was wrong with my car. "Well, there's a sort of quiet shwooshing sound from the back, then there's an almighty twang, the car shudders a lot and then carries on as normal." From Trevor's previous expressions I know that he is a master interpreter of shwoosh and twang. It would be so much easier if I could say "the main differential over the manifold has warped alongside the bottom sump" but then if I could say that then I would probably also know what the problem is. For what it's worth I have no idea if what I've just said even makes sense, they're just terms I've heard bandied around from time to time.

Of course there are other times when words fail simply because you don't know what the problem is. My friend's cat is unable to eat at the moment, several expensive X-rays later and they are still none the wiser and none the healthier. There is nothing as distressing as not being able to even offer a guess. "Seems happy, but can only lick the food." If only they could talk as a rather famous veterinarian once commented. It seems daft to suggest that a cat is "not quite himself" but anyone who has a pet knows what they mean and thankfully vets tend to know that if you have a hunch that something is wrong then invariably you are right. Sadly though the malady is often not found. Even worse is baby's crying especially if it's your first. The amount of times I would look at my eldest in despair trying to decipher the unholy wails from the tiny bundle. Some doctors also seem less helpful than vets. For some reason most vets I have encountered accepted that I knew what I was talking about with my cats but many doctors would give me the patronising look reserved for new mums. The idea that my concern for my son was somehow a nuisance or detraction really shook me. I took advice from my mother who asked whose opinion I valued more, mine or theirs and what did I consider to me more important, my child or their timetable? As soon as she put it like that my doubt fell away and we finally got the situation properly diagnosed. Thankfully it was a one off case but it took a long time to sort out.

Of course most of the time in the early stages I and thousands of other parents would look at their wailing charges in desperation. They were fed, they were clean, they had just slept for hours, they were the right temperature, they had no rashes or sore neck (I would always go straight to Meningitis) so why wouldn't they stop crying? Please. Please stop crying. For the love of god stop crying. Of course I soon calmed down, sleep deprivation has the bonus of turning you into a mind numbed zombie and I soon accepted that sometimes babies just like to have a good old howl. If only he could have turned to me looked me in the eye and said "Now see here Mother, you are doing a great job and I want for nothing but I am currently feeling the need to express my inner turmoil with my role within the universe." Life would have been so much easier but as has been so often in my life, words failed me.

Happy birthday to Us!

It's our birthday! Hurley Books first started formally trading in November 2002. A website called Amazon had just opened up part of its site to second hand sales. Steve and I knew all about books and about selling them, I was a librarian and he had supplemented his college years by selling books on market stalls and fairs. Being a librarian I was pretty clued up on how important the internet would be and so I suggested that we gave it a go. At eleven o'clock that night Stephen dashed into the bedroom. Now given that our two boys were one and three my sleep was precious to me and unless there was a problem with one of the children this had better be good. In Steve's eye it was better than good it was miraculous. We had just sold a Mary Jane Staples for £5.87, a book he could only ever sell for £2.50 on the market stall. I was less than impressed, I knew it would work, we see it all the time in libraries. People love their authors and are desperate to read everything by them, once a book goes out of print it becomes harder for them to read. Simple supply and demand. At this point both our eyes glazed over, mine through exhaustion and Steve's through amazement.

Since then Hurley Books has grown quietly and slowly. We were able to give up our jobs and we opened a little shop, below a dentist's, in St Austell. People began to walk in through the front door. We began selling face to face as well as online. After a year the dentist needed to expand and we moved to Charlestown. Now I have to say, hand on heart that I have never enjoyed my job so much as when I was perched on a wooden stool listening to Seth Lakeman and looking out over the tall ships and the sea beyond. I could have happily sat there, day in day out, the most contented person ever, without seeing a single customers but once again (thankfully) they turned up.

Finally we took the plunge and in a high risk strategy (well for us anyway) we bought our own place in Mevagissey and took on a warehouse in Par. Suddenly we were shop owners and our home no longer looked like the British Library. That was five years ago on December 2nd.

Mevagissey has been a great success for us; it's given us stability, income and a great sense of community. Each year we have tried out new things to stay ahead of the game, bookselling is not an easy business at the moment and last year, in December again, we launched The Cornish Bookshop, a website focusing on Cornish books and the like. I'm thrilled to say we have loads of support for this venture and I'm looking forward to seeing how it develops.

So we are nine years old; we have been in Mevagissey for five years and the Cornish Bookshop has passed its first milestone. Now, it goes without saying that we couldn't have done it without you so we are most cordially inviting you to come and join us Saturday 3rd, EV Thompson will be with us signing his new book and we'll be serving mince pies and wine throughout the day. Call us to reserve a copy. Fingers crossed the scaffolding will be down and you can admire our newly painted shop as we put on our best bib and tucker. It's also the Christmas Lights in Mevagissey that day so there'll be loads of things going on. Please come and join us, it wouldn't be the same without you!

One for the birds

This week seems to have been one for the birds. On Saturday, Harry and I went for our regular rugby stroll down to Polridmouth beach and along the cliffs when half way down I began to hear a shooting party coming from the Menabilly estate area. I wasn't that bothered as Harry is unaffected by loud bangs, fireworks don't faze him, two screaming boys don't faze him so why should some distant guns. As we got closer to the beach he hared off into the undergrowth and came back proud as punch carrying a dead pheasant. Nothing for it now but to head towards the guns and return one of their birds, it was so funny watching Harry trot past the Labradors and proudly drop his find at the feet of the shooters. It's a strange way to see birds up close when they've just been shot but I'm afraid I'm not sentimental about it, I eat them and they taste great.

Which is just as well because on Monday, Dave dropped in a brace of pheasants and partridges to the shop. Oh good I thought as I eyed their splendid plumage, how the hell do I prepare a whole bird. In the end I chickened out and just removed the breasts. I know it was a bit wasteful and I had some great casserole and roast recipes in front of me, but one of the birds still had grain in its gullet and it was all a bit too much. When I was younger I couldn't enter a butcher's because the smell of blood would make me very queasy but like most things you just learn to suck it up. Not the blood, that would just be gross, in fact I'm making myself queasy again so I'll move on.

Having dealt with the birds I had to dash off to get the boys so I wrapped the four birds in newspaper, popped them in a bag and dashed off. It would be hard to describe the slaughter house scene that greeted me and the boys on my return. In a rare show of co-operation the cats and Harry had got the bag off the table onto the floor and then opened it up. Blood, feathers and body parts lay all over the floor, table and chairs, three living animals looked very pleased with themselves and four dead ones looked even deader. My boys just stood there looking on in shock! Harry tried to look nonchalant but was unable to pull the look off properly as he had feathers sticking out of his ear, the cats just looked at me as if to say "and?"

Moving away from game triumphs and disasters I've also had a great week bird spotting. This is a perfect time for it as there are no leaves on the trees and branches and so the birds can't hide so easily. Obviously bird spotting isn't so easy with Harry, I usually just see the backs of birds as they fly away in alarm but sometimes I get lucky. On Tuesday morning a walker told me to keep an eye out for a kingfisher, the man had seen it every day for the last week at this spot. I have to say I haven't seen it once! I have seen lots of others though, chaffinches, goldfinches, curlews, chiffchaffs, pipits, turnstones, stonechats and maybe a cirl bunting – this last one is unlikely as they're not supposed to be around here but it really didn't look like a yellow hammer which is the next closest thing it could have been. So there we go, if I haven't been massacring or inventing them I've been spotting or eating them. Hope you enjoy our feathered friends as much as I do.

A sports stadium for Cornwall

Well we didn't beat St Austell but we didn't lose either. Like many close games, there was a certain level of dissention over decisions and there were definitely frowns on both sides of the pitch, depending on which way the decision went. The week before against Saltash was no better, in fact it was worse; we were winning, then Saltash scored the winning try and the final whistle was blown immediately after (by the ref who was also a Saltash coach.) I'm not saying anything. As the light fades so too do the sailing, surfing and golf to be replaced with cross country running, football and rugby. Nice, clean sports to filthy, dirty, mucky sports. My poor washing machine.

All this talk of sport has made me think about the current call for a sports stadium in Cornwall. It almost seems too much to imagine, which I think shows the level of the problem, if we can't imagine it, how can we ever realise it? The reason I can't imagine it is quite simply the cost. We're such a poor county, the government is skint so who exactly will pay? These things cost a fair few pennies, always seem to go over budget and probably won't be ready until my grandchildren are up and running and given that my children are only just up and running I'm hoping that happy event is a decade or two away!

A stadium offers all the obvious sporting benefits but it also offers others that aren't instantly thought of. It offers health benefits and employment ones and for some children it will give them the break that school can't provide. Schools by and large are set up for academic, not sporting excellence. This will be a new venue for some children to thrive and realise that Cornwall cares about its athletes as much as its academics.

It can also host social events, gigs and concerts. We know from the Boardmaster Events and the Eden Sessions that over 60% of the audience come from out of county so there is no problem about being able to fill a stadium, especially if the names are big enough. The trick is to make a stadium pay for itself and wipe off the debt as fast as possible; using it for a variety of functions is the way to do it, including some top ticket price attractions.

A stadium also has a community benefit. Steve and Finn regularly travel to Plymouth to watch Argyle get beaten but agree that it would be so much better to support your own local team in decent facilities nearby. It would also be nice to watch a win once in a while but apparently being a fan isn't about the winning? There's something special about a good stadium that really lifts the teams and the crowds. When I lived in Cardiff, home matches were played at Arms Park, literally just a road over from the city centre. When Wales scored a try, the whole of Queen Street would reverberate to the noise from the stadium. It was quite a memory to be popping in and out of shops accompanied by 20,000 Welshmen. Sitting in a local pub listening to the match on the radio or tele was done so with a live backing track of the stadium roaring in approval. There's a moment when the whole community would stop and grin at each other as they realised that Wales must have scored a try as the air echoed with roars, and for a second they were all brought together, before carrying on with their day to day tasks.

So all in all why wouldn't we want a stadium? Let's hope that the money can be found and the right location agreed upon and then the sky can ring out to the cries of "Come on Cornwall!"

Every wants a piece of me

It's all going to hell in a handcart! Global warming has arrived ahead of schedule, first class stamps will soon cost 60p, the Government want to put VAT on my pasty and it cost me £80 to fill up my car yesterday. To be honest I've taken to looking at the sky to see if it's falling down yet. I'm not sure what concerns me most, the VAT on pasties is a bit of a red herring but the whole VAT issue is one that affects my business so I'm watching this story with care. The postage hike is more immediately alarming, not because of the price hike, which is a concern but because it is the first step in making the Royal Mail ready for privatisation. I don't mind paying a bit more for a fairer price but I am alarmed by the idea of the postal service becoming privatised.

I could be sarcastic and comment on how well privatising the rail network and the water companies worked, to say nothing of the benefits in privatising the electricity and gas companies but what would be the point. None of us actually think that it worked out for the best. Where we are stuck with a local provider, as in water, we are facing the highest costs in the country because we have the beaches that the rest of the country makes use of for half the year. Where we have a choice of providers such as the power companies they have ensured that the tariffs are so confusing that no one is capable of getting a good deal and keeping it. If we want to travel across our nation we run the utter headache of multiple timetables and pricing structures that can make flying to Greece cheaper and easier than taking a train to Haverfordwest.

So nationalising the post office? Bleugh. Great for the cities – obviously but for rural areas, far flung areas, islands? This is going to hurt. The whole strength of a nationalised industry is that the strong helps the weak and we truly all pull together. And can you imagine the mess when a book fails to get delivered, every company along the network will be able to blame each other. At least if I put a letter in a letter box now there is only one place to turn to if it fails to arrive.

So long term it's the Royal Mail that bothers me as it will have a noticeable impact on my online business but what concerns me the most at the moment is the ever rising cost of fuel. My tank tends to last me a few weeks and yet every single time I go back the price has gone up again. I sold my gorgeous old petrol guzzler because £50 a tank was outrageous. Now I'm putting £80 into my fuel efficient diesel and it doesn't seem fair. I mean really £80 and I'll need to do that again in three weeks. I could buy a lot of stuff for £80 that would last a damn sight longer, shoes, clothes and so on. I really don't know how people are managing and that's what concerns me the most, soon something has to give, our cars are not luxury items they are essential parts of our daily lives. So despite the sunshine I'm a wee bit fed up today. Oh well soon it will start raining and then I'll have something new to complain about! Enjoy the sunshine and catch up next week.

We're just a little bookshop

Now some of you observant readers may, by now, have realised that we have a bookshop. In Mevagissey. Near the harbour. Hurley Books it's called. I was thinking the other day that in 10 years of trading we haven't had many celebs buying their tomes from us. The more I thought about it however, the more I realised that I was wrong. We've had our fair share. Probably the most well known was Griff Rhys Jones who called into our shop when we were in Charlestown to buy a local guide.

Steve once served the lady who co presents "How clean is your house" on TV. Aggie MacKenzie. He didn't recognise her of course, probably because she is a middle aged woman who presents a cleaning programme and has no connection with football. After she had left and I told him who it was his only comment was "Oh, do you think we passed?" Probably not.

We've yet to get a film star in, although Johnny Depp was a distinct possibility when he was filming in Charlestown. As was Mel Gibson when he, allegedly, paid a visit to the area when directing "Apocalyto". They both evaded our clutches, clearly not big readers.

There has been the odd brush with royalty. Prince Edward's wife was in Mevagissey recently and walked past our shop. She even looked in but, alas, did not cross the threshold. We did once send a book, ordered on the internet, to Buckingham Palace. It may have been ordered on behalf of the Queen so who knows we could be by Royal Appointment? We also send out to some pretty famous names via our online business. However, given that I am Liz Hurley a name doesn't necessarily mean what it might suggest.

And let's not forget the infamous. Several times have we sent books to prisons. I have no idea what the purchasers had done to land themselves in jail but what better way to pass the time than with a good book. Perhaps the thickness of the book is an indication of the crime. "War and Peace", must be in for high treason, "Animal Farm" must be a looter. We've also sent a few to the Houses of Parliament but I wasn't sure whether this group belonged to the former or the latter category!

The crème de la crème, though, are the literary celebs. They may not be as well known but we, in the book trade, tend to get dewy eyed when authors come a callin'. The real joy of authors though is that by and large we don't know what they look like and that's the sort of fame I like, respected for what you've done, not what you look like.

That said it's rumoured that Brad Pitt is in Cornwall and desperate for something good to read, so why not come down to our shop. You may catch a glimpse of him.

Let's meet those low expectations

So Eden marks its tenth birthday and has brought billions into the SW economy over that decade. I guess I've got laid back about it but that's an incredible achievement! I'm so used to it being on my doorstep and yet it really is a global building and it's here in Cornwall, just down the road. I see that Tim Smit's next project is also going to be in the St Austell area and is going to be a water therapy park. I can't wait to see what he does; will we be swimming in the gravel pits? Watersliding down the pyramids? Lots of seaweed wraps scooped up from Par beach? Given Heligan and Eden whatever it will be it will be a success and another total asset for Cornwall. Great things can happen when one person has a vision and has a team backing them up. Where things tend to go wrong is when they hit committees. "If Columbus had an advisory committee he would probably still be at the dock". Let's hope that Smit manages to get his next project past planning without too many hiccoughs, after all his track record speaks for itself.

I was really disappointed to see the article in last week's West Briton about the rejection of Prince Charles's design for a new housing estate. One of the main problems was that of the centre piece construction, a Georgian style crescent building. This building would have provided many of the 97 homes, 35% of which will be affordable, either for rent or first time purchase. Some of the reasons for the rejection were because the building would have been "overly ornate" and "too grand". A new, scaled down more subdued building has now been put forward. How incredibly depressing is this, too grand for Cornwall eh? Should we all know our place and keep looking down. What's wrong with aspiration? Talk about paucity of expectation. Are scrolls and columns not for the likes of us then? Let's keep things plain and quiet, let's not rock the boat by doing something that might attract attention.

Can you imagine how wonderful it would be for someone going into their new council home and discover it was a place of beauty. People live up to their environment, time after time it has been shown that if you give someone somewhere nice to live they stand taller (I'm excluding teenager's bedrooms from this you understand). I've driven through Poundbury many times (HRH's development outside Dorchester) and it's wonderful – everything looks good, traffic moves slowly as pedestrians have right of way and there are little corner shops everywhere selling all sorts of things, it thrives and buzzes and loads of it is affordable housing, that's a council estate that I'd give my eye teeth to live on.

I'm not saying that the new designs for Truro aren't nice; it's just frustrating to hear that something is too grand. This is a stunning county, with incredible people who have shaped this nation and the world beyond, through their endeavours and inventions. Nothing is too grand for Cornwall, and Cornwall deserves nothing but the very best. I know we are a poor county, disadvantaged and overlooked by central government but for someone in Cornwall to say something is too grand is terribly sad. It's like being stabbed in the back by your own side.

Is a kindle the end of the world?

I would imagine that most of you out there in reader land have heard of a website called Amazon. It started out as an online retailer of books and now sells most things. It is a very powerful and very successful phenomenon. For the past two years its bestselling product has been the kindle. The kindle, for those who don't know, is a wireless reading device. Put simply, in terms even my husband can grasp, you download books, via a computer, onto your Kindle and then read them at your leisure. Turning the page on a kindle is a swipe of the screen. It can hold up to 3,500 books, weighs 247g and has battery charge of a month. It is, we are assured, the best thing since sliced bread – although a slice of bread is a bit heavier and thicker than the kindle.

It may be no coincidence that independent bookshops are closing at a rate of knots and that Waterstones has announced poor profits and is looking to close 20 stores across the country. Could this be the death of the book, or the publishing industry as a whole? Well I don't know, it was a rhetorical question, but I do know that the kindle is not for me. I like gadgets and gizmos as much as the next person but a book should be read as, well, a book.

There is something wonderful about browsing for a new book to read, picking it up and flicking through it, turning to a page at random and reading a sentence or two. A book has a certain smell, a certain feel and looks good on a shelf. A good book can bring back some happy memories. I still have the book I read on a holiday to Jordan. There is still sand between the pages and Dead Sea mud fingerprints. All my old university books are proudly on display, complete with spidery handwritten notes in the margins. And rereading a favourite is like meeting up with an old friend. I would imagine reading a book on a kindle is a bit soulless.

But for us it's not just about reading books, it's also about selling them. So, are we tightening our belts? Are we looking with a gloomy eye to the future? Is the butler's job safe? I suppose time will tell, but for now it's onwards and upwards. Who knows, there might be a burgeoning market in second-hand kindles in a few years' time. With a bit of fanfare and a re-launch we could become Hurley kindle. Trips off the tongue nicely... maybe these kindles aren't so bad after all.

Ode to Joy

I am currently going through the rather noisy introduction to Led Zeppelin, they were a bit before my time so whilst I've always recognised some of their music I was never a fan. My house now resounds though to Robert Plant screaming and wailing through the floorboards as my eldest has suddenly discovered them.

I was pleased to be able to tell him that if he liked Led Zeppelin he may also like The Who. Apparently someone at school said Zeppellin were a lot like Abba, so it's nice to see that when it comes to music I am at least better informed than one 13 year old. Although if put to the test on current music I imagine they would thrash me.

The funny thing is a few years ago Puff Daddy did the theme music for the film Godzilla and completely lifted Zeppelin's Kashmir beat. At the time, when I pointed this out to Thomas, he was full of derision, what did I know about Puff Daddy? Furthermore if there was an old fogies song in there it was Puff Daddy that made it awesome. I reminded him of this conversation the other day but unsurprisingly he had no recollection of it. Mark Twain once wrote "When I was a boy of 14, my father was so ignorant I could hardly stand to have the old man around. But when I got to be 21, I was astonished at how much the old man had learned in seven years." This is a regular occurrence in our house.

Music seems to be the preserve of youth but I don't think that's quite fair. Certainly they have more time to listen, discover and create music than someone trying to work nine to five and run a house and all the other boring grown up stuff but I don't think we love music any the less. I used to fall in love with a track and then play it 10, 20, 30 times in a row. I still do and I don't think I'm alone in this because my ipod has a little repeat button that means a track can be looped eternally. I'd like to think I'm pretty important in the eyes of Apple but somehow I don't think they've added this piece of software for just one compulsive addict. Lots of us must do it.

In fact I have to say I love my ipod and youtube, suddenly I am surrounded by music again and discovering new stuff and tracking down barely remember tunes. Many's the time that I'll be out walking with Harry, my headphones on and the perfect random song choice comes on. It's not uncommon to spot me break out into a little arm waving samba and two step on top of Carn Grey, and many a seagull has been startled by the bellowing of Nessum Dorma or just me laughing to hear "Running up that Hill" exactly at the moment when I am, indeed, running up that ruddy hill.

Music is something that resonates very, very deeply into our memories, moods and personalities. The power of it is widely known as it is a well-respected form of therapy and it certainly cures me. So if you've got out of the habit of listening to music, stick something on and brighten your day.

The new online world

I often used to wonder how people living though the industrial revolution felt, or how the introduction of cars and electricity changed things. Did they look around them and go wow! Was there ever a generation that didn't say "it was tougher in my day, you kids don't know you're born!" For what it's worth I think we are going through a massive worldwide revolution at the moment, as dramatic as the collapse of the feudal system or the changes wrought by the Industrial revolution but this lurch had been heralded by the microchip and has happened in the blink of an eye. Previously revolutions have taken place over many decades and filtered slowly through countries and population but the one we are in now! Within one generation the world has turned on its head. My boys don't understand how we didn't have a computer at home when we were small, but how did you do stuff? When my sister went to Australia we didn't hear from her from one week to the next, we relied on the post and haphazard and very expensive phone calls. Now the boys keep in touch with their mates wherever they are on the globe via Facebook and the like. Tribesmen in various African countries consider their mobile phones as essential items; before they walk 40 miles to market they can ring ahead and find out which market is offering the best price. Mobile technology is revolutionising the world but had barely been around 30 years. From my phone, I am in touch with the whole world.

New communications and communities are emerging that could never be imagined before. We started as online traders and indeed that is still where the majority of our business is focussed but that's a career that we could never have had when we first met. I'm back· in touch with my cousins who I haven't spoken to in years, scattered across the globe the way they are. Now we chat, share laughs, swap photos and we're all hoping to get together in August.

I'm talking to people I've never met before but I have to say the online community is a bit odd. Devoid of personal contact and only being able to communicate through type, meanings are mistaken, offence is easily caused and jokes miss the point. I decided to try out this online community first time on the R4 Woman's Hour chatroom. Big mistake, enormous mistake. One of the posters had voiced an opinion on stay at home mums when another "lady" rebuked her quite harshly. Now, I don't like to see rudeness or bullying, even if it is just in type and I was thinking of this poor poster sitting at a computer somewhere typing her opinion only to have been publicly lambasted in the chat room. So I typed a few friendly words of support to her. Again in public, all these chats are done publicly. Next thing the former "lady" went for me. She was savage and deranged, what would I know about anything, what the hell gave me a right to an opinion, how exactly had I suffered? And so on for about a paragraph of vitriol. I replied saying she was unpleasant, signed off shaking and never logged into Woman's Hour again. Bruised and confused I tried a chatroom for booksellers where again I was almost instantly attacked for having a stupid name and told to wait a few weeks before venturing opinions. I'd only said Hello! Thankfully, lots of other posters quickly jumped in and told the attacker to shut up, welcomed me and said that as this was an open site all were welcome – even the bullies. I've remained chatting on this site for years now and have picked up lots of industry knowledge and helped share some of my knowledge gained from mistakes. We even have get togethers around the country to meet up in person. Everyone has online nicknames and many's the time I've made incorrect assumptions about people, be it their age, sex or race. In a way it's quite liberating, the only thing you know about the person is what they type, there are no clues to wealth, class, ethnicity, gender, age and so you learn to type with care, to try to avoid assumptions and not to boast or lie.

I spend a huge part of my day on the computer, in fact without it I wouldn't have a business, it is essential to my ability to make money but it's also a very sociable tool. I belong to various online networks which again, is a concept that didn't even exist a few decades back.

There's an e-mail network for Cornish business women that I am part of, we share skills knowledge and experience as well as asking for help. I don't know who any of these women are but if I have a query I throw it out there and e-mails come flooding back in with advice and suggestions.

Technology is running and not all of us are keeping up, some of us don't have mobile phones, let alone "smart" phones, no pcs at home no access to the internet at work and it's easy to forget that for some it's easy to feel out of place. It will be interesting to see how we progress over the next few decades and to see if society shapes technology or technology shapes society.

Exploding stupid cars

What a week! First a friend dragged me out clothes shopping because I turned up to a party in a man's DJ. When I said I had nothing to wear I wasn't joking. I have no dresses; everything I try on looks awful so I have nothing. Jo refused to believe that this was possible and dragged me to Truro where I tried on over 50 dresses, I am not exaggerating, and it was terrible. Some of the dresses made me look like a dowager, many of the dresses made me look like I should be standing on a street corner, others made me look like Bibendum's fatter cousin but eventually through her persistence I started to find the odd few dresses that looked good and in the end I bought two. One will probably go back but I was so tired at the end of it that I just couldn't choose.

Monday then descended into what I thought was a tooth abscess but turned out from the x-rays to be just bad sinusitis. Just! Pain ensued. Tuesday the car died. My alternator belt snapped, flew off, got tangled up in the cam belt, shred the cam belt which in turn destroyed the engine. All in the space of about 10 seconds. I was quite impressed that a car could disintegrate so dramatically so quickly.

Now the rest of our week has been all about me having a lousy headache and cold, trying to transport dogs, children, books around the place in just a two seater van and our rather desperate hunt for a new car. We obviously need a bit of a work horse, it's our only family car, we have boys who have lots of kit, in summer bikes and surf boards hang off it. In winter it fills up with mud from football and rugby matches. We regularly travel to Wales and Norfolk in it and other places in between. It needs to house two dogs as well as two boys and quite often cases of books. So like I say; a work horse. It also needs to be fuel efficient. Ha. It needs to be cheap. Haha. And Steve would like it to be new. Hahaha! Younger son has requested a Humvee, eldest feels a Koenisegg would be better. I'm wishing we had more money. Honestly having to buy a car just before Christmas is galling.

What it comes down to is that we will have to buy a banger and keep our fingers crossed that there is lots of life left in her, unlike our sons we are not petrol heads so we don't care what we drive around in just so long as it's cheap, reliable and can keep up with us. Very tempted by a London Taxi that I saw for sale, nice and cheap however the insurance is astronomical but wouldn't that be fun? Would love to have another Volvo estate but there are none around at the moment in our price bracket. Also loved our old Mercedes but we sold the last one because although it was very cheap to buy and an absolute dream to drive the running costs were abysmal. Of course I'll never touch a Passat again, I think we just got unlucky with this car's constant electrical faults but once bitten.

So at the moment I am going to go to my fancy Christmas dinner tomorrow in my fancy new dress with a streaming head hold and arriving in a van. Oh the glamour!

What makes a perfect school?

The children were asked what would make a perfect school and I thought how different a school could be depending on who was asked.

If I was a child my perfect school would be one where all my mates were. I'd be allowed to play and chat whenever I wanted to. There would be no homework and the lessons would be interesting. I would like to be top in my class at everything but if I couldn't be, I wouldn't want to be laughed at. I also wouldn't want my teacher to shout or sneer at me. I'd like a decent lunch-time with nice food and then enough time to play. I'd like my school to be nearby so I didn't have to spend all my time on buses. I'd like longer summer holidays and fewer exams. As I get older I'd like the teachers to notice and stop treating me like a baby and appreciate that my hormones are absolutely out of control, as is my ability to be awake at 9.00 a.m. And when I pass all my exams I want people to say "well done" not "exams are easier these days."

If I was a teacher my ideal school would be one where I was valued. My boss would support me and back me up, as would my staff. I would be well paid to reflect how important what I do is and I wouldn't be mocked for always being "on holiday". When I entered a classroom it would be great if there was silence, it would be lovely to have a class of students ready to learn. It would also be nice to know if my students could speak English or if they had been moved care homes the night before. It would be nice not be called a "stupid b**ch" it would be even nicer that if the name calling was reported, that disciplinary action might take place. I'd really love to be able to teach a subject the way that I knew worked. I'm sure I would get very fed up at having to take on a new teaching style every two years to reflect a new   government policy. It would also be great if the   examination system could just stay the same. I'd also not like to be judged by double standards, if my pupils fail an exam then that's my fault but if they pass an exam then the system's too easy.

If I was a parent I would like my child to leave school believing that they could rule the world if they wanted to. I would want them to look back at school as a happy and enjoyable time; I would also want them to have learnt useful and interesting things. It seems that it's too much to ask but if they have a cookery lesson I would like them to learn how to cook rather than how to assemble a salad and design a wrapper for a pasty. I wouldn't want my child to be so stressed by the idea of failing to get 30 A* GCSEs that they can't sleep night after night. I wouldn't want my child to see drugs in their school and teachers being sworn at. I would want them to be safe from intimidation from other pupils and I would not want my child to come home to tell me how much their teacher shouts at the whole class the whole time. I'd like them to do more games and sports and more homework. I'd like the school to keep in touch with me and let me know how my child was doing. I'd also want the school to have greater power to dismiss bad teachers before they ruined my child's brief stay at school.

The one thing in common would be that whoever I was, teacher, child or parent, I would want to be treated with respect. Now, how do we go about achieving that?

Looking pretty not stupid

With Christmas fast approaching I'm having fun watching the beauty adverts. Yes, I know I need to get out more. Like any advert that is about to employ "science" to sell you something, advertisers seem to lose the plot. Out come the white coats, the ridiculous claims, the invention of new breakthrough product, *hydrolipo-polyannates*. They're all breakthrough by the way. I mean Pantene now comes in a water based formula – well thank god for that, I can finally throw away my acid based shampoo and that Gastrol conditioner was doing nothing for my locks, so thank you Pantene for inventing this revolutionary product. Oh no, wait a minute, that's right, that's rubbish. All shampoo is water based, it's the first principle ingredient, only they don't call it water, it's aqua. Aqua sounds more scientific, more chemically, more expensive. I'm not going to pay £4 for a tub of water but a tub of aqua, why £4 is a positive steal!

I know I mock and as Steve will tell you I'm right at the front of the queue for fancy pots of lotion, I enjoy it, nice smelly creams and potions are fun but it doesn't make me stupid so I don't appreciate being treated as such. Do you remember that awful ad with Jennifer Anniston doing a hair or skin advert when she uttered the atrocious line "Concentrate, here comes the science bit" Huh? Because I wash my hair does that make me the intellectual equivalent of a dung beetle, if I clap my hands, do I miss? What is the correlation between beauty products and stupidity? And before you men try to jump up and answer that question can I draw your attention to the recent "male grooming" adverts? It appears that you poor chaps have been neglectful of your skin, all that snowboarding, bmx-ing, rally car racing, boxing and late night poker nights are hell on your dermis, but don't worry L'Oreal knows that when you play tough you need Hydra Energetic. No, it's not moisturiser, that's for girls; this is Hydra Energetic, totally different. Really. Honestly. Ugh!

It's like the coke adverts. Diet Coke is advertised by dolls in a fashion agency, Zero Coke however is in a black can. It's cool. Again it seems to be drunk inbetween boxing, snowboarding and driving cool cars. If you check their website they agree that there is a slight taste change between the two products but both have the same level of calories and sweeteners. Clearly the advertisers realised that men didn't care about their weight but liked the idea of all that cool snowboarding!

I don't know if this blatant targeting of men is a step forward or a step back. I suppose it's nice to see that men are also being treated as idiots by the advertising agencies and it's a far cry from the Brut adverts, although that Old Spice advert did also go in for a lot of surfing. Women seem to sit around looking pretty whilst men go out and do stuff. Exciting stuff. Stuff that involves boards or mud or white water. When they start advertising rugby players using Hydra Energetic then I'll be impressed but I can't see it happening. Mind you Gavin Henson would be the ideal candidate.

So I don't see what's wrong with a bit of prettiness and pampering. Why should frills and ribbons have something to do with IQ, why should the love of pink denote lesser brain power? Because I'm not prepared to be patronised by a gender that believes the loo roll fairy changes the roll over, that isn't aware that the lid on top of the laundry bin is actually removable and that cups hidden behind curtains won't go green with mold.

So Steve, if you read this a gift pack from Clarins will do just nicely and I'll continue to tackle the laundry bin on my own.

Rubbish!

Well it's all rubbish really! That's what the past few weeks seem to have been all about, I'm not talking metaphorically but actual rubbish. It all started two weeks ago when I was woken up by the almighty crashing of glass. I ran to the bedroom window where I saw the new recycling van coming round to collect the new bags and boxes, if it was a minute past seven it was only by a hair's breath. I had two thoughts, the first was that that wasn't the nicest way to wake up, the next was even grumpier as I realised I had missed my collection. I am so used to putting out my bins when I wake up (seagulls and foxes – I know – only in Cornwall) that I hadn't realised that the recycling rounds would start so early.

Anyway this morning I was up at six and duly put out all my bins, bags and boxes, startling a deer that ran off down the road – a very surreal start to the day I have to say. I was hoping that the crash of all my wine bottles didn't alarm the neighbours too much but I needn't have worried, it's nine o'clock now and no one has collected them yet. I also needn't have worried about getting up at six o'clock but then I'd have never seen the deer. It's sccms though that I am one of the lucky ones as some people are having their recycling rejected, are not having rubbish collected or don't have the new bags yet. I hope it all settles soon and I am in favour of it but it is a bit of a fag trying to find a place for all these large bags. Still if it's a bit of a fag versus landfill pollution I can cope with the former.

My next encounter with rubbish was the incinerator debacle at St Dennis. I mean how long do those residents have to keep fighting? Burning rubbish is rubbish. It is the last word in wastefulness and it will cost a bomb to build. Nothing about the incinerator makes sense to me. If we can't produce enough waste to burn because we are all recycling instead, then SITA can import waste from other counties to burn. Wonderful! Lots of lorries driving up and down the motorways carrying rubbish. Absolutely barmy.

Finally I was having a chat with someone and he was telling me about a chap that drives to a lay-by has a cigar or two and then empties his cigar tin etc. on the floor and away he goes. Fundamentally this is the problem isn't it? Not land fill management, not what day and time our bags are going to be picked up but bottom line, do we really care what we do with our rubbish. You can't walk five minutes anywhere without seeing rubbish. Our hedges are festooned with poo bags, the curbs have fag ends and paper cups in them, our beaches are awash with plastic bottles and crisp packets. And it's not a holiday maker issue, this happens all year round, too many of us just couldn't care less. There's a place where I park with Harry, it has a litter bin but every time I go there the car park is littered with rubbish,

I often see local residents picking up the McDonald wrappers and the tins of beer and putting them in the bin that is within five metres of the rubbish but why couldn't the person who threw it out the window not have done the same thing?

A Cornish Brigadoon

Do any of you live in the area between Lanivet, Lanlivery and Luxylyan? It's a lovely area with Helman's Tor sitting right in the middle of it but you have to admit if you don't know where you are going it's a hopeless maze of little lanes going round in loops with no need for road signs.

My reason for being there was that I had discovered a new walk for Harry, there's a wildlife area there called Brenney Common. Almost impossible to find unless you know where you are going but great if you persevere. Harry and I have been really enjoying the new scenery and so I thought I would drag Steve along as well, he works too hard. I had almost managed to convince him to come for a walk with me one morning when I got a rather panicky call from my youngest son. It turns out that whilst he had successfully got himself onto the train he had failed to get his school bag on quite as successfully. This resulted in Steve spending half an hour on the phone trying to get in touch with St Austell station and me dashing across town to retrieve the bag and drive it down to Truro. For the record, you can't phone St Austell directly, that spoils the system. Apparently, central office takes care of everything, right down to the fact that any left luggage is automatically put on the next train to Bristol lost property! I ask you, how daft is that? Anyway when I arrived a lovely lady called Nicola had guessed that it was a school bag and that some harassed mother would be arriving shortly so she held onto it. Thank god for common sense, no matter how unwieldy or stupid the system is it is still run by humans with common sense and fair play.

That rather put the dampeners on the walk and in the end Harry and I took a turn around Idless Woods by Truro. The following day we tried again and I dragged a reluctant Steve out with me. We had a great walk, well there's no such thing as a bad walk but then I could see him twitching to be back at work so we jumped into the car and set off. We had gone one mile when we met a lorry unloading building supplies, we waited with patience and increasing exasperation and finally we got past him only to meet a tractor, unloading sheep or turnips or something, I have no idea I was four cars back. After 10 minutes and a rather impatient Steve I reversed along the lane found a turning and zipped off again, only to meet a car coming the other way. After a bit more reversing we were on our way again only to be stopped at the level crossing for the clay train. I kid you not! At this point I figured I would never get Steve to come on a morning walk again. Finally I dropped him off and headed home. On my way I was stopped by a tree feller, two sets of traffic lights and one road works. Next time I want to travel five miles I'll set out the night before

Writing and reading for The Cornish Guardian

I don't know much about you, in fact I know just about nothing about you but the one thing that I do know is that you enjoy reading the Cornish Guardian. This Christmas I got the chance to actually sit down and read the whole thing cover to cover and really enjoyed myself. It's always a shame though that the property section of the Christmas edition is so light. If there is one thing I love about the paper it's flicking through the property pages and choosing my next dream house, in a sense I'm glad I'm not rich because I'd be spoilt for choice, how would I decide between 20 acres of moorland or beach frontage?

The Christmas paper is also unusual in that we get to read the writings of the other local columnists. I think the people of Bodmin, Lostwithiel and Looe are well served with their columnists and it's nice to see the standard I have to try to keep up to, it's also nice to see what is going on in the other areas beyond the standard news stories. One place that is great to find out what is going on is the letters page. This is the section that I always turn to first because it makes sense of the news stories and also has the bonus of some days making me laugh out loud. Last week we had the treat of a councillor getting in a huff because praise for some scheme hadn't been duly allocated to him but to a fellow councillor. His letter was full of "me, me, me" and outraged indignation, this week was even better when the second councillor retaliated saying that the first councillor was misguided and that HE was the one who did all the work, in a rare case of one-upmanship the councillor backdated his claim of interest to when he was a "young lad". I have never read two letters more full of their own self-importance. I'm looking forward to a letter in next week's paper from a councillor claiming to be Spartacus. It is funny but really guys, you're councillors. Is this seemly? Is it helpful? Does it matter? Surely the bigger picture is that the event was a success?

Like their letters, I often find that I'm at odds with the political columns none more so than Dick Cole. He always writes eloquently and persuasively but I generally find myself disagreeing – not this week though – how could George Osborne suggest creating "low pay zones" for public service workers. The only decent wages in Cornwall tend to be in the public service, we should be trying to raise everyone up to their pay and working conditions not pull them down.

Another letter that struck a chord was from Keeley Allen, who volunteers at a local animal shelter. They want to employ her but have no funding, she wants to work for them and stop claiming benefits so the pair of them have written in asking if anyone knows where they may get funding for £5K a year. I don't know the ins and outs of this story but it comes across as one of those situations where you think the system just isn't working. By the same token Keeley is trying to fix it, so good luck to her and I'm also keeping my fingers crossed for Marna who is still waiting to have her furniture fumigated. Her letter was informative, polite and nicely ironic, I have no doubt that the people at Ocean, who really do care about their residents, will have sorted out the glitch by now. So that's my review of last week's paper and I hope you enjoyed it (the paper) as much as I did.

It's beginning to look a lot like Christmas

Apparently it's beginning to look at lot like Christmas but not in our house, at the moment we are a house of lurgy with sick cats, dogs, children and me. I wouldn't normally be so concerned, other than surprised that everyone is ill at the same time, we're usually a pretty robust lot but the fact is that Christmas is just around the corner and I'm nowhere near ready. We were all going to my mother's for Christmas but due to an appalling set of circumstances everyone is now coming to ours

My poor mother had only just moved into her new cottage when the landlord told her that her lean-to was going to be repaired. What has followed has become a laughable catastrophe. It seems that they decided to take the roof of the house off instead, they failed to secure the tarps properly and then we had all that heavy rain two months ago. Suddenly Mum had a shower in her bathroom, unfortunately not the normal type but rain water coming in through the ceiling, over the weeks as the builders failed to return, the shower moved to both bedrooms and the boiler. As she put it, she was a bit fed up one night to realise that the plip-plops in the various bucket were now being joined by a new shower on her pillow. So for a while she was sleeping on the downstairs sofa. When the leaks started to get into the kitchen she was finally able to convince the landlord to send in an electrician to check if the wiring was safe. At the time he condemned the electric shower, pointed out that the storage heaters didn't work but that the kitchen seemed fine. Once he left the rain started again and fresh leaks sprung up everywhere. She tried to light a fire but the smoke from the chimney filled her neighbour's living room so that was out. The roof has now been fixed, after nearly three months but there are still leaks. She has no hot water as the boiler was rained on and she doesn't know if it's safe, the landlord hasn't been back to check on electrics. She can't use any electrics at the back of the house because she's so concerned about their safety. The tiles are falling off the bathroom wall because the plaster has blown. She has only one storage heater in the whole cottage that just about works and so she is living in a cold and damp house. Understandably we can't do Christmas at hers and she's fed up. Not only has she had to throw things away because of water damage but she just wants a warm, dry home where her children can come for Christmas. When you're in your 70s it's not too much to ask is it?

So not only is she fed up but so am I. Why is it that if all you can afford is the lower end of the housing market, then that means that you receive the very worst sort of care and service? Her landlord won't answer her calls or that of her neighbours, the builders are the worst sort. If she could find warm, dry and affordable housing she'd be gone in an instant but she's stuck where she is. I know Christmas is a jolly time and I know Mum's situation could be a lot worse but things like this really remind you that too often as a society we ignore the poor, the old or those that can't fight for themselves. Like I said I'm not feeling very Christmassy at the moment. Give me a week and I'll be glass half full again.

Merry Christmas

With the weather forecasters beginning to mutter about heavy snowfall I wonder if we are going to get a white Christmas? Beyond the romantic notions of a white Christmas it just seems right. Winter should be cold; there should be snow otherwise what makes it a season distinct from the others? We're heading up to Dorset to be with Steve's family, it's going to be a house heaving with brothers and sisters, cousins and aunts, grandparents and cats and dogs and I suspect by the 26th I will be heading towards a breakdown.

I know Christmas is a time to get together, to be with friends and family, to relax and have fun but honestly I can have lots of fun in a silent house, with sole command over the radio and TV, I'll have that bottle of beautiful port all to myself and I won't have to share the terrine. I'll take the dog for a two hour walk along the cliffs without a backdrop of complaints and I'll get to watch Doctor Who without my niece hanging off my ear and my father in law telling me how good Doctor Who is whilst I try to watch it. He's loves it as much as I do but seems to be able to watch it and talk through it, without it hampering his enjoyment one jot. It's clearly a failing of mine that I can't.

I'll go to midnight mass and sing my heart out without the embarrassed murmur of offspring looking mortified. I'll have smoked salmon and champagne on Towan beach for breakfast and will not be dragged away to open the presents.

As it is I'll experience 48 of the noisiest hours of the year. There will be no respite and no silence but there will be lots and lots of laughter. There's bound to be tears as the cousins are young and there'll also be cries of "cheat" as once again we all try to fleece each other at cards. The fleecing becoming more and more apparent as the bottles fill up the bins. I doubt we'll go to mass and I imagine all the presents will be opened in an ecstasy of fumblings before 8 a.m. Greg will take control of the TV remote and we'll all be subject to Jamie telling us how we should have cooked the turkey. Steve's sister Sarah, known to all as Roo, will grin with evil pleasure as Greg and I look on in horror when Jan puts the sprouts on at the same time as the potatoes. Then she'll thrust a glass of something festive in our hands and who cares? I suspect Sarah also pines for the silence. And whilst I know this all sounds manic I'm also really looking forward to it.

So whatever your Christmas is, I hope it's a good one. For those of you on your own, enjoy the peace and silence, for those of you with family, enjoy the company, for those of you working, I hope that everyone you work for treats you with extra gratitude, for those of you that don't celebrate Christmas I hope you enjoy the break and for those of you for whom Christmas is a rough and difficult time I hope it passes soon.

Have You Read...

LOSING IT IN CORNWALL

The second collection of essays from Liz Hurley. If you liked this lot then you'll love the other book as well. Currently available from Hurley Books in Mevagissey, or on Amazon as a paperback or a kindle.

GIVE US A REVIEW....

In order to keep this book selling it needs lots of great reviews on Amazon or Good Reads. Good reviews help heighten the visibility of my books and allows more people to see it on their list of recommendations.

KEEP IN TOUCH...

We're on all the usual places, choose your poison and come and join us.
www.facebook.com/mudlarkspress
www.twitter.com/mudlarkspress
Instagram: and_then_it_exploded
https://uk.pinterest.com/hurleybooks/

LOOK OUT FOR MORE GREAT BOOKS FROM MUDLARK'S PRESS COMING SOON...

Mudlark's Press

Mudlark's was established in 2015 in a response to the nightmare of getting my first book published. In the end it seemed easier to do it myself, and whilst it actually wasn't easy at all, it was fun. Coming soon are a book of walks, a guide book and a children's storybook. After that? Who knows? Maybe you have something?

Mudlark is a family nickname and it felt nice to bring it out into the light. We have nothing to do with the Thames!

Made in the USA
Charleston, SC
02 November 2015